HEART

and

HEAD

OTHER BOOKS
BY DWIGHT N. HOPKINS

Introducing Black Theology of Liberation

Shoes That Fit Our Feet: Sources for a Constructive Black Theology

Down, Up, and Over: Slave Religion and Black Theology

Black Theology USA and South Africa: Politics, Culture, and Liberation

*Black Faith and Public Talk: Essays in Honor of James H. Cone's "Black
     Theology and Black Power"* (editor)

Religions/Globalizations: Theories and Cases (coeditor)

Liberation Theologies, Post-Modernity, and the Americas (coeditor)

Changing Conversations: Religious Reflection and Cultural Analysis
     (coeditor)

Cut Loose Your Stammering Tongue: Black Theology in the Slave Narratives
     (coeditor)

We Are One Voice: Essays on Black Theology in South Africa and the USA
     (coeditor)

HEART

and

HEAD

Black Theology—Past, Present, and Future

DWIGHT N. HOPKINS

palgrave

for St. Martin's Press

First published 2002 by PALGRAVE™
175 Fifth Avenue, New York, N.Y.10010 and
Houndmills, Basingstoke, Hampshire RG21 6XS.
Companies and representatives throughout the world

PALGRAVE is the new global publishing imprint of St. Martin's Press LLC Scholarly and Reference Division and Palgrave Publishers Ltd (formerly Macmillan Press Ltd).

ISBN 0-312-29383-6 hardback

Library of Congress Cataloging-in-Publication Data

Hopkins, Dwight N.
        Heart & head : Black theology—past, present, and future / by Dwight N. Hopkins.
            p. cm.
        Includes bibliographical references and index.
        ISBN 0-312-29383-6
        1. Black theology. I. Title: Heart and head. II. Title.

    BT82.7 .H664 2002
    230'.089'96073—dc21   2001048213

A catalogue record for this book is available from the British Library.

Design by planettheo.com

First edition: February 2002
10 9 8 7 6 5 4 3 2 1

Printed in the United States of America.

For my daughter—
Dora L. T. Hopkins

CONTENTS

ACKNOWLEDGMENTS

Many people have read all or parts of this book or have provided opportunities for me to speak on these ideas. Some have been kind enough to spend time discussing the various analyses and proposals. I thank J. B. Banawiratma, Will Coleman, James H. Cone, Valerie Dixon, Ramathate Dolamo, Gary Dorrien, Michael Eric Dyson, Diego Irarrazaval, David Jehnsen, LeAnne Jones, Patricia O'Connell Killen, Emmanuel Lartey, Rita Lester, Tinyiko Maluleke, Manning Marable, Joerg Rieger, Ana Maria Tepedino, and Emilie M. Townes. My wife, Linda E. Thomas, offered critical comments and enthusiastic encouragement throughout the writing process. A special thanks goes to Gayatri Patnaik, my editor at Palgrave. From her initial suggestion about my doing such a book through the final touches on the manuscript, Gayatri has truly been a writer's editor. Very early on she saw the potential and necessity of black theology engaging crucial concerns of a broad audience. She has been an intellectual conversation partner, a technical production person, a gentle nudger, and an ongoing affirming voice. Without her initiative and support, this project would not have come to fruition.

Finally, I wish to acknowledge reprint permissions from Orbis Books for the included essays on method and womanist theology modified from my *Introducing Black Theology of Liberation* (Maryknoll, NY: Orbis Books, 1999), from Taylor and Francis LTD (http://www.tandf.co.uk) for the included modified version of my "Globalization and Black Theology" (*Peace Review: A Transitional Quarterly,* vol. 7, no. 1, 1995), and from Duke University Press for my "The Religion of Globalization," *Religions/Globalizations: Theories and Cases,* eds. Dwight N. Hopkins, Lois Ann Lorentzen, Eduardo Mendieta, and David Batstone (Durham, NC: Duke University Press, 2001).

All of the essays in this book were presented at different times and in different contexts.

Dwight Hopkins's Vision

by Michael Eric Dyson

Dwight Hopkins has emerged over the last decade as one of the most prolific and insightful thinkers among the second generation of black theologians. Taking his cue from mentor and black theology founder James Cone, Hopkins has sought to clarify the relation between faith and the struggle for social justice. His books have always crackled with first-rate scholarship, and his arguments are always framed by a compelling logic. But what is especially appealing about Hopkins's lucid explanations of black religious belief is his grounding in the wit and wisdom of his forebears. Hopkins has never been afraid or ashamed to delve deeply into the folk genius of black culture, whether it surfaced in a slave narrative, a backwoods sermon, or the earthy eloquence of a community elder. Hopkins has helped to expand the intellectual gestures and scholarly impulses of first generation black theologians and religious thinkers—besides Cone, they include figures like Vincent Harding,

Jacquelyn Grant, Gayraud Wilmore, Albert Cleage, Henry Mitchell, William R. Jones, Charles Long, C. Eric Lincoln, J. Deotis Roberts, Joseph Washington, and Preston Williams. The first generation black theologian and religious thinker worked diligently to legitimize the theological and ethical interpretation of black oppression, finding their sources in both sacred and secular culture, from sorrow songs to blues ballads. The second generation of black religious intellectuals—led by Hopkins and scholars like Cain Hope Felder, Josiah Young, Katie Cannon, Delores Williams, Emilie Townes, and Theodore Walker—has dug into the suggestive terrain of black popular culture, folk narratives, and African heritage. Hopkins has been particularly keen on challenging the divide between sacred and secular in black life, highlighting the theological insight found in folk tales, blues songs, short stories, novels, autobiographies, work songs, toasts, testimonies, poetry, and even gossip.

Heart and Head extends Hopkins' theological reach by making his thought more accessible to a broader audience. Hopkins manages the feat effortlessly but, more crucially, without losing his critical acumen. The range of themes he tackles in this book bode well for the future of black theology. Hopkins begins boldly, enlivening black theology by emphasizing its womanist meanings. By giving pride of place to the varieties of black female religious experience—and criticism of male dominated thought—Hopkins performs the theology he professes: the womb of ancient wisdom, so long denied, is honored as an important source of his theological vision. It is refreshing as well to note Hopkins's insistence that spirituality be explored within the scholarly boundaries of black theology. If spirituality is what we feel about transcendence, and religion is what we believe about God, then theology is what we think about what we feel and believe. To be sure, this formulation does violence to the complexity, and frankly, the subjectivity of the terms discussed. Still, the importance of spirituality, so long relegated to second-class theological citizenship, is rightly uplifted in Hopkins's thought. The same is true for his common-sense admonition against exhausting the concept of gender when referring to women. Like whites who forget they have a race, men forget they have a gender, and one that favors straight identities at that. In one fell rhetorical swoop, Hopkins dismantles the logic of heterosexism by giving a human—and dare we say, divine—face to gays and lesbians. Dismantling, it appears, is an edifying tool in Hopkins's theological arsenal. He ingeniously takes apart the idea of globalization as a religious force—examining its constituent elements while suggesting that a real theology of liberation must help its adherents actively resist the all-consuming ideology globalism spawns. But when he takes away, Hopkins also gives back. In this case, it is a wonderful analysis of international ecumenicity that turns religion from the water of social habit to the wine of authentic fellowship for liberating purposes.

Hopkins's grand theme—indeed, his magnificent obsession—is one he inherited, then brilliantly elaborated: the restoration of justice to the poor. His treatment of James Cone is at once festschrift and refinement of an idea that Cone has passed along; namely, that God sides with those whose backs are against the wall, whose options are severely curtailed by poverty, whose identities—as blacks, as women, as sexual minorities—are the source of social inequality. What Hopkins does superbly is take up his mentor's charge by exploring just what an option for the poor looks like, how it shows up in theological garb, and what it might say about the possibility of true community. It is beset by the fractious intrusions of racism, sexism, economic inequality, sexual dysfunction (which is what homophobia really is), ecological terrorism, bias against the young and old, emotional imbalances, and bigotry against two-thirds of the world, since people of color are a majority of the world's population. It is Hopkins's insistence that we view the world through the lens of the oppressed, especially the victims of economic injustice, that connects us to our forebears. Still, he ranges valiantly across intellectual boundaries by joining forces with cultural critics, social theorists, and political analysts in the fight against injustice, thrusting black theology into richer theoretical vineyards and deeper scholarly wells.

The appearance of *Heart and Head* is not only auspicious but providential. We are at yet another nadir in our culture—remember even stalwart figures like Harry Emerson Fosdick were momentarily seduced by the gospel of wealth and health in the last century—where narcissism and materialism literally gang up on poor believers and masquerade as true belief among the ecclesiastical elite and many of their flock. Hopkins's book is a salvo in the war to reclaim justice and sacrifice as the heart of the gospel. His book could not have come at a more desperate time, giving vital support to the efforts of thinking people of faith as they attempt to vanquish the idols of unmitigated prosperity and material excess from within the camp of belief. With televangelists touting the virtues of immediate gratification; with local churches growing by leaps and bounds with a gospel that coddles and encourages the undisciplined pursuer of consumer goods; and with myopic biblical justifications for the acquisition of personal wealth abounding in self-help bestsellers, Hopkins's voice is a pathway out of the theological mess in which we are mired.

At its core, *Heart and Head* is a passionate and profound book that makes the best of its play on the similarly-titled classic in black religious letters: Howard Thurman's moving autobiography, *Head and Heart*. Like that volume, Hopkins's sharp and illuminating book helps his readers clarify their thinking about hugely important issues that loom large in black—and American—religious life.

Risking a New Future

I don't remember much of the funeral. I do remember a couple of my older brothers crying. It seemed so strange. Although I had seen both of my older sisters shed tears at home, I had never seen any of my five older brothers cry. And now a couple of them were bawling out loud in public. I hardly remember seeing much of anything else during the service. My oldest sister had smothered me in her lap, covered me with her arms, and bathed me with her tears. I do remember talk about the rocklike faith of the deceased and how, if it hadn't been for segregation, she easily could have gone to college—she was so gifted. She possessed an undying thirst for education and had been a member of her church choir and active in Bible study classes. It was 1962. I was nine years old, and this was my mother's funeral.

When my mother died, my father was suddenly responsible for eight children. Some of my mother's family began to discuss the possibility of taking care of the two youngest children: me and my next oldest sister, Brenda. But it never crossed my father's mind that anyone else would ever take care of his sons and daughters. He had brought them into this world and he would make sure that they received the proper faith and education to prepare them for life. My father's commitment to the dispossessed and disenfranchised was strong, and his religious faith on behalf of the vulnerable stemmed from his conviction that one required both the heart of compassion and the head of education to know what the right action was for any situation.

In 1976 I began to reflect on what my father had endured since his birth in 1907, and especially since he became a single parent. I marveled at this black man growing up in the postslavery South who lived so long and cared so deeply for his children. I wondered why he and my mother had raised their children in the church, and one day I approached him to discover his reason. I asked him why he never remarried, since he surely had ample opportunity—I had seen different women in the neighborhood stop by the house and leave food and desserts as gifts for him. He responded that he never remarried because he was committed to spending his time and focus on raising his children. My soul swelled inside of me in awe as I listened to my father articulate his determination to love his own family as his vocation of service. How, I asked, did he get to the point where he was not fazed by the hardships in life? He replied that he was born a southern Baptist in rural Virginia and his was that old-time religion where God would fight your battles and give you the victory. And when you fought, you had to understand that God helped those who helped themselves. Religion didn't mean anything, he concluded, unless it meant helping people less privileged than yourself.

I remember my father talking of his amazement at the young people today who have access to so many educational resources. But they don't seem as smart as the old folk of his generation in some ways, he observed. Because he had to work in the fields and cut wood, he only reached the sixth grade. Yet his life experiences and commonsense wisdom, from his birth near the turn of the twentieth century until today in the twenty-first, gave him enough knowledge to earn him a Ph.D.—and more. Sitting there listening to him advocating for the necessity of education in the younger generation, I recalled the moments he praised me for my grades and school activities when I had lived with him in the 1950s and 1960s, and I remembered when he brought me my first very own dictionary. In fact, the two most striking memories of my father were when he acted like a cheerleader for my intellectual activities and when he worked around our house while singing "This little light of mine, I'm gonna let it shine. Jesus gave it to me," a religious song created by black people.

It was in conversation with my father that I realized that two of the greatest gifts from my parents were faith and education. A faith of service to the less fortunate in the community and a spirituality of justice for the most vulnerable people went hand in hand with a disciplined and determined approach to education. Sympathy for those living in poverty and those suffering at the bottom of American society complemented the purpose of education and belief. A compassionate intellect and an intellectual compassion were two sides of the same coin. The heart, or faith, inspires and strengthens a vision of a new society, while the head, or education, tells us what to do with that strength in order to fulfill that vision.

This realization affected me so profoundly that, after graduating from an elite Ivy League college, I walked away from the possibility of earning joint JD and MBA degrees at that same university. Instead, I opted for community organizing in Harlem, New York, which is one of the largest black communities in the United States. If faith connected to service, and education clarified faith in service, then my own privileged education obligated me to be with people who lived every day in structural poverty. Poor people do not own any economic wealth—they work for others or are chronically unemployed, exist at the lower end of the income ladder, and barely survive day-to-day. This structural poverty is a permanent feature of capitalism because the increase of wealth at the top of society results in an increase of material poverty at the bottom. This redistribution and concentration of wealth upward is not an aberration or accident. It is a normal part of a capitalist economic structure. The spirituality of the heart enabled me to have compassion for those worse off than myself. And the analysis of the head allowed me to understand how black people were forced into poverty and to think about what resources they could use to get themselves out.

From 1976 to 1981, during five years of serving the inner-city black community, I continued to feel a deep spirituality of justice and an ongoing thirst for increased formal education. One day while eating soul food in a Harlem restaurant during the summer of 1981, my closest friend casually handed me a two-page article that was copied on pink paper. The essay was titled "Left Strategies Must Deal With Racism." My friend was aware of my southern upbringing that focused on education as service and on the black church as the place for involvement in the plight of oppressed communities. Since we had been schoolmates at Harvard, he knew how long I had struggled to combine a black liberation spirituality with the highest intellectual activity. Like me, who had spent five years at an all boys' New England boarding school, he was an alumnus of a similar prep school. And so he appreciated directly the anxiety in my soul. This dilemma had possessed me. Wasn't there something that came out of the African American tradition that satisfied both the heart and the head, so that poor black people, and all working people, could live without a few elite families monopolizing all the wealth in the United States?

Initially I didn't even read the article that my friend gave me or note who the author was. But I took it home and dutifully filed it away. About a month later something moved me to search for the essay. I read it in full, and it is no exaggeration to say that from that instant on, my soul became rested.

"Left Strategies Must Deal With Racism" was about the tradition and vocation of a black faith that genuinely took those who live in structural poverty seriously. It was a well-argued statement showing deep faith in the black church and in black spirituality. Clearly, the author was one who loved working-class African Americans and saw the need for the church to live on behalf of them and, through them, all peoples. The author unleashed a sharp criticism of ostensibly progressive whites who say one thing but are just as racist as some of the more outspoken advocates of white supremacy. In addition, the article enjoined us to take up the cause of the people of Africa and other parts of the Third World. It's difficult to convey just how engrossed and excited I was by this essay—all I remember is that it seemed like I read it in about sixty seconds! I immediately went back to the beginning for a second reading, this time studying each sentence deeply and poring over each word. Instantly I knew I wanted to be part of this movement.

Up to this point, I hadn't even looked to see who had written this article. The caption under the picture of the black man with the Afro read: "The Rev. James H. Cone is Professor of Systematic Theology at Union Theological Seminary, New York City." Finally, I thought, a black man who was a minister, a professor, and who took seriously the class realities of the majority of African Americans—the working class and poor. I had lived in New York City for five years, but I had never heard of Union Theological Seminary, nor had I heard of James H. Cone—and I certainly had never heard of systematic theology. Although I felt anxious, I knew something larger than me was calling me to risk a new future, so I looked up the phone number for Union Theological Seminary, and after what seemed like extraordinarily long rings, Professor Cone actually picked up the phone. I was thrilled. He invited me to his office in Brown Tower for a meeting.

Unbelievably, Union was literally four blocks from the tenement I had lived in as an organizer in Harlem. I had walked past and around the buildings of Union numerous times but never knew that the school existed. When the day finally arrived, I was simultaneously exhilarated and anxious, bubbling and cautious, bold and fearful.

When we finally met each other, it felt like coming home: We talked and talked and talked. Cone asked me many questions: about my history, education, visions, life experiences, interests, commitment to black and other poor people, and future plans. I, in turn, asked him about the article I had read and about what he believed. It was there that I first heard of and began to learn about black theology of liberation. The more he spoke, the more I saw myself in the tradition, history, and picture that he painted. I was so engrossed and committed that after several hours of discussion, Professor Cone and I agreed that I should go downstairs and enroll in the Master of Divinity program, which would start in a couple of months at Union. He indicated that, because it was so close to the beginning of school, I would not have any scholarship or fellowship monies the first year. Despite any financial hardships, I was still excited about studying the connections among justice, faith, and service at Union.

I went to see James H. Cone because of a sense of a spiritual calling that had gripped me and led me. When I crossed the threshold into his office, I had no intention of enrolling in Union Theological Seminary. In fact, I had never heard of an "M.Div." degree. But I left Union that day as a student registered for classes. After three years of the M.Div. program with Cone, the founder of black theology, and after four years of completing the Master of Philosophy and Ph.D. degrees with him as my advisor in systematic theology, my life was changed forever.

BLACK THEOLOGY — FREEING
THE SOUL OF THE NATION

Black theology is the interplay between the pain of oppression and the promise of liberation found in the Bible, on one hand, and a similar existence experienced by African Americans and poor people today. Since their arrival on the shores of the "New World," people of African descent have always maintained a sacred sense of life. But this religious view of the world faced its most severe threat when white Christians introduced a form of the Jesus story calling for Africans and African Americans to obey their white earthly masters as they obeyed their "white" heavenly master. From 1619 to 1865, the period of slavery in the United States, religious whites used Christianity to justify the dehumanization of black folk in chattel and to bolster antiblack racism. In other words, Christianity was white supremacy. But based on their memory of West African ways of being equal creatures before their High God, Africans and African Americans reinterpreted Christianity as the champion of the oppressed sectors of society. In the Bible, they found the thread of liberation of enslaved Hebrew people and connected this narrative with the Jesus parables, which emphasized the healing and liberation of the outcast and of people forced into material poverty.

Since the beginning of slavery until the early 1960s, African Americans forged a foundation for a new way of believing in and living out, on Earth, the good news of Jesus. They developed different aspects of a new spirituality and religion, but they did not carve out a complete and comprehensive theology. In a real sense, the definition of *theology* contrasts with those of *spirituality* and *religion*. Spirituality is what we feel, need, and do spontaneously—an almost natural belief in some person, force, being, or thing greater than the human situation or mortal capabilities. And religion comprises the rituals that institutionalize the practice of spirituality. Theology, however, insists that we pause and critically consider what we claim to believe and how we act. It serves as a critical reasoning and as an intentional sorting out of the human spontaneous feeling of dependence on something more than human efforts. Theology moves us to think systematically about the nature of our faith, spirituality, religion, and the God–human connection. This is why theology is called systematic and constructive theology.

How do all the aspects and questions of faith fit into a constructive, comprehensive system that links us to the Jesus story of liberation of the poor, our sacred traditions, and the struggle to be fully human in the contemporary period? Only in the 1960s did a specific black theology of liberation come forth to map out a response to these questions.

Black theology, a pioneering liberation theology indigenous to the United States, started in the global context of a shift in world order, particularly after World War II—the second major violent conflict on European soil in the modern era. A combination of international and domestic factors came together to provide the backdrop for the origin of black theology in the mid-1960s. So too have the emerging world order and related North American developments posed novel problems and new possibilities for black theology at the beginning of the twenty-first century.

Certain international dynamics after World War II promoted the dawn of the African American civil rights and black power movements of the 1950s, 1960s, and 1970s. These two currents of resistance, which helped launch many other domestic human rights struggles for equality during this period, were the foundation for rethinking the theology of African American churches and other faith communities. Black theology did not fall willy-nilly from the sky but burst onto the North American domestic scene (and globally, at least in South Africa) through a combination of local and international influences.

The postwar era positioned the U.S. government and its monopoly corporations as the undisputed champions of capitalism and American-style democracy in the noncommunist world. It also had an immediate effect on 1950's black civil rights efforts in the southeast United States. Black Americans supported this seductive ideology of liberation from fascism and communism. These systems were based on either racial superiority (such as Nazism) or human rights violations (due to state dominance). If the world's greatest government had stopped Hitler's blitzkriegs and fought to make the world safe for democracy, then surely this same government would soon resurrect its own black citizens from the death of racial apartheid at home.

The rhetoric and worldview championed by North American power structures abroad were taken very seriously by African Americans fighting against white supremacy and voting discrimination at home. But when black soldiers came back home, reality soon set in. Blacks began asking how the U.S. government, which apparently seemed so sympathetic to people millions of miles away, could neglect, if not oppress, its own black citizens—many of whom lived a stone's throw from the White House. And so an evolving postwar debate about freedom, democracy, and equality helped give rise to the civil rights movement.

Indeed, talk of a better world did help start the African American mass efforts for justice. But so too did the concrete reality of thousands of black Americans who fought abroad against Nazism and biological supremacy; it made an incredible imprint on the historical experience of collective black America. African American GIs returning from tours of duty abroad after World War II and the Korean War had accumulated firsthand knowledge of the world, especially about racial relations. They learned that it was possible for white working-class youth from Mississippi (Ku Klux Klan country) to live, work, sleep, and play with black working-class youth from backwoods Georgia.

The two antagonists could reconcile their differences and function as equals in the midst of waging war for a higher cause. All the white eugenics theorists, all the social determinist professors, all the propagandizing politicians, and all the white theologians had been wrong, absolutely wrong. Life experiences proved not racial irreconcilability but rather racial unity grounded in a justice goal.

Black soldiers abroad felt free for the first time, relative to their home experiences. The only segregation the French sought was to identify and isolate the hated brown shirts. Unless instigated by American whites, the word *nigger* did not pass from the lips of white Europeans when they saw a black person in one of Uncle Sam's uniforms. On the contrary, black soldiers felt so liberated while in Europe they even experimented with interracial relationships with French and other white European women. Unlike in small-town Alabama, no cries for lynching were heard.

To be seen by whites of Europe as simply other humans was a revolutionary education for black GIs. The unthinkable—that divine creation, mental intellect, cultural incompatibility, natural antagonism, and human tradition did not prevent black and white equality— had occurred. Discharged from duty, African Americans reentered civilian life in the United States determined not to let Jim Crow turn them around.

The domino effect of global decolonization also fanned the flames of black church–led civil rights initiatives and the black power challenge. African American communities and churches were well aware of the struggle for self-determination being fought by brown, yellow, and black peoples in the international arena. As early as 1938, for example, numerous black churches rallied to defend Ethiopia from Italy's invasion. India's independence from Great Britain in 1947 conveyed some of the first signs of hope. Mao Zedong's wave of red guards successfully moved the People's Republic of China out of the capitalist orbit in 1949. And starting with Ghana's independence ceremonies in 1957 and Nigeria's in 1959, European colonial administrations in Africa gave way to indigenous ruling structures.

World War II so captured the attention and resources of European colonial powers that it gave nations on the global, political, and economic periphery an opportunity to assert themselves as independent actors. Thereafter, the Cold War between the United States and the Union of Soviet Socialist Republics further opened the crack of opportunity for newly developing nations.

Two other dynamics helped nurture the civil rights and black power movements and, in turn, the birth of black theology. One was the 1954 U.S. Supreme Court decision that declared separate facilities for blacks and whites as inherently unequal. The *Brown vs. Board of Education* decision emerged partly from a reassessment of the world theater by the U.S. government and its multinational corporations. To expand post–World War II American hegemony, it was necessary to modify the apparent contradictions between domestic apartheid—violent structures against black people sanctioned by the federal administration—and U.S. rhetoric about America being the land of opportunity. However symbolically intended by some, the decision nevertheless provided a major incentive for African American struggles for citizenship and full humanity.

The last factor was the Marshall Plan. This post–World War II scheme allowed American multinational firms to penetrate Europe and helped boost the American economy back home. Like other Americans, blacks experienced rising expectations about their education and standard of living. As a result, the belief that each generation of children would improve beyond the lifestyle of their parents increased tremendously. Global macroeconomic realities suggested national microeconomic expectations. The international payoff of progress for white Americans spurred the impatience of African Americans domestically.

Against this global backdrop, black theology emerged from the work of a group of radical African American pastors and religious educators whose faith challenged them to link Christianity and the black struggle for social transformation. It was an attempt to redeem the soul of and reorganize the North American system. By July 1966, black theology was closely linked to both the civil rights and black power goals of racial equality and real democracy.

Those movements drew on a long tradition: African American people have always organized for a more rewarding life—if not for themselves, then eventually for their children. This quest was accelerated by the events following World War II. Since the days when American white Christians held blacks in slavery, the African American church has been unsurpassed in leading the resistance.

And so when one of the most momentous justice movements in the twentieth century—the civil rights effort—began in 1955, it was led by the black churches and symbolized by a black Baptist preacher. The Reverend Martin Luther King Jr. combined black slave theology (that God is justice, protest, and freedom), national liberation movements (the move of underdeveloped countries toward self-determination), Gandhian nonviolence (thus expressing solidarity with the formerly oppressed nation of India), and the lofty ideals of the U.S. Constitution and Declaration of Independence.

King's theology and African American church practice were new. They made the fight for freedom the defining objective of Christianity and called upon faith communities to actively change the world, even at the risk of physical harm. Consequently, Americans could not call themselves Christian if they violated the full humanity of other human beings. This was a revolutionary change from the prevailing American Christianity that had promoted instead the ideology of profit and individualism.

The appearance of black power, symbolized by the resurrection of Malcolm X's thought after his February 1965 murder, constituted the other half of the emerging black theology. While the civil rights initiatives linked Christianity with justice and church militancy, the black power movement situated the cultural identity of blackness at the center of any real justice for African Americans. That meant the right of self-identity: the right to name one's black and African self independent of white control; and the right of self-determination: to control black communities unhindered by white power. Unlike the civil rights effort's limited terrain, black power swept every region of the country and affected every quarter of the African American community.

For certain groups of black pastors and religious educators, the black power goals represented the very heart of what it meant to be a Christian. "Secular" black power advocates, following Malcolm X's legacy, sneered at Christianity as the white man's religion. In response, black theology arose in July 1966 to wed the radical black self-reliance of the black power advocates with the freedom message of civil rights. Black theology identified Christianity for the deprived of society—that is, the civil rights way of life—with the call for a black cultural and political renaissance—that is, the black power way of life.

In the 1960s and 1970s, black theology centered the concept of "liberation" within religious and theological dialogue. This language developed directly out of the national liberation speeches and slogans of Third World nations, both nonaligned and socialist, as they called for national independence against (white) colonial powers. Similarly, black theology was the first religious movement to clearly equate Jesus Christ with the liberation of the oppressed in North America in the struggle against (white) domestic power. It did so because African American theologians were heavily influenced by national liberation fronts that were fighting against (white) colonialists around the world.

In the language of global resistance organizations, *liberation* had an exact meaning that was adopted by black theology into the Christian conversation about protest for equality. An oppressed nation, by the standards of both the United Nations and the former Communist International, had the right to separate from systematic restrictions that victimized its people.

Third World nations were unified by a common language, territory, culture, tradition, and (perhaps) racial or ethnic stock. Drawing on the grammar of international organizing for independence, black theology combined this talk with a Christian framework of Jesus Christ the liberator. Although not all black theologians advocated an absolute separation or independence from America as the final goal, all agreed that blacks had the right to self-identity—that is, name change, African culture, linguistic style, slave tradition, racial lineage; the right of self-determination—that is, controlling their destiny and communities; and the right to separation.

"Black theology of liberation" is the name given to a movement created by a group of African American pastors in the late 1960s who felt that the gospel of Jesus Christ had a positive message for black people despite the negative racial conditions they faced. The National Committee of Negro Churchmen (NCNC) and, later, James H. Cone believed that the good news of Christ called for a ministry in which God and human beings would work together to transform this oppressive social condition into a new community of justice on earth.

Although the ministers of the National Committee of Negro Churchmen were the first group to give a religious interpretation of the black power movement in 1966, it was James H. Cone, an ordained African Methodist Episcopal (AME) minister and professor, who wrote the first book on black theology. In that work, *Black Theology and Black Power* (1969), and in his second book, *A Black Theology of Liberation*

(1970), Cone redirected the entire course of religious thinking in the United States. His writings were bombshells dropped on the abstract and irrelevant definitions of mainstream theology. Cone stated that the essential message and work of Jesus Christ was to liberate those living in structural poverty. Thus, the African American struggle against racism and poverty sided against the rich and white supremacy and fought for the material and spiritual liberation of people at the bottom of society. For Cone, Christianity was not alien to black power. Indeed, black power was in itself the contemporary manifestation of Jesus Christ.

These earlier works of Cone proved to be extremely significant for the continuing growth of the black church as a viable alternative for African American progress. Before his publications, many in the African American community saw the black church as irrelevant to black freedom. They perceived the religious thinking or theology of Christians as an opiate focused on heaven, while the white community enjoyed their heaven on Earth. Because Malcolm X and the Nation of Islam spoke so clearly on this position, they had cut deeply into the membership and recruitment of black churches. But Cone offered a resounding "yes"—Christianity was completely compatible with black consciousness and black power. The African American struggle for freedom is totally equal to the full humanity of black people as expressed in their faith in Jesus Christ. Calling for a return to the black church, his writings lucidly articulated the necessity of linking the progressive culture and liberating politics of African Americans with the core mission of the church. In this way Cone laid the theological groundwork for black survival and resistance. Consequently, his books and articles helped to bring an entire generation of African American youth and young adults back into the church.

In addition, Cone's writings decisively changed many justice minded people's way of thinking about religion and human social conditions in two other ways. I believe he was the first person in the history of the United States to position liberation of the poor as the central and foundational preaching and teaching of Jesus. With this theological analysis, no longer could one be a Christian without organizing one's life around the well-being of the vulnerable in society. And Cone was one of two people in the world to first write books on liberation theology. Gustavo Gutierrez wrote his *Toward a Theology of Liberation* in 1969 and his Spanish edition of *Teologia de la liberacion* in 1971.

Black theology was needed, argued Cone and the National Committee of Negro Churchmen, because all theologies are human speech about God's relation to humanity. Contrary to what too many mainline white churches preached, God does not do theology; people carry out this project. Humans exist in particular cultural and political contexts, and, therefore, their theologies are not objective but rather are subjective movements interested in different sections of society. Since the gospel of Jesus Christ is essentially one of liberation for the disempowered in every community and because human social relations in the United States were characterized both by racial discrimination against African Americans and by their struggles toward freedom, black theology of liberation was needed not only for African Americans but for America in general. By removing racial obstacles and negative social hierarchies blocking the God-given rights of poor black folk, progressive peoples had a better chance of equalizing wealth and democratizing politics for all. With this process expanding, justice and peace could reign throughout the United States.

Theologically, black theology of liberation states that God created this world for all humanity. But hubris or selfishness has led most of the American white community to hoard God's created order for themselves. Therefore, in black theology evil encompasses both personal and systemic sin. To fight such a sinister force, group account-ability, individual responsibility, and personal individuality are all required. In addition, evil has existed in the monopolization of power over resources and over divinely given rights or privileges for all humanity. In the American context, this denial of equalizing power has shown itself in the disproportionate number of African Americans suffering from disenfranchisement on two levels. First, racial discrim-ination has denied the positive self-identity of what it means to be a black person, especially in the context of the U.S. apartheid structures of the 1960s, where the definition of what it means to be human was encoded by law and by custom in the identity of white Americans. Consequently, blacks were not seen as human beings—thus erasing both their African heritage and their unique gifts of being black people on North American soil. Stated simply, to be human was to be white.

Second, in addition to restrictions on positive self-identity were restrictions on African American people's right to self-determination. All peoples, particularly poor communities, were given the right to deter-mine for themselves how they wanted to conduct themselves on earth—how they attempted to control wealth, resources, and the space surround-ing them. Because the image of God in us is total liberation and grants freedom in a total manner, the first component of black theology spoke to cultural concerns and the second to a political agenda. If the church followed the stories of the Bible, then it was essential to work with Jesus in the midst of the movement to realize self-identity—as in black cultural rights—and self-determination—as in black political rights—in the African American community. In sum, black theology of liberation arose as a Christian movement of freedom for the transformation of personal and systemic power relations in American society at the point of racial difference. Unfortunately, today many suffer from a form of historical amnesia, which leads them to perceive black theology as another trendy intellectual discipline, simply another theological course to be taken at the undergraduate and graduate school levels.

Fortunately, beginning in the early 1980s, a second generation of black theologians has arisen, including younger African American thinkers who seek to explore theology from any and all aspects of reality. These trends illustrate black theology deepening its ties both in the black church and in master's of divinity and doctoral programs. A slowly increasing number of African Americans are attending graduate schools of divinity, theology, and religion, and they are institutionalizing themselves in the American Academy of Religion—a national organization of scholars, all of whom possess some doctoral degree related to religion. The Society for the Study of Black Religion likewise remains a vibrant intellectual location for African American religious scholars. Similarly, the ties between black churches and black professors have deepened with more scholars either pastoring, copastoring, or working in and with churches in some capacity.

Furthermore, today's black theology is finding more research and publications centering on primary African American sources—for instance, slave narratives, folk culture, music, biography, and public policy. Afrocentrism, which attempts to remove Europe as the center of black sacred life and replace it with Africa, is adding its mark to the purpose of African American theological concerns today. Also, the founding or first generation of black scholars from the 1960s persists in publishing and pacesetting various parts of black theology, especially in the areas of pan-Africanism, spirituality, African American religious history, and the commonsense wisdom of black leadership. And a small cadre of black educators and ministers are openly establishing their lesbian and gay identities as gifts from God and, therefore, directly challenging black theological beliefs.

THIRSTING FOR A NEW HUMANITY

The challenges of the twenty-first century demand an ongoing black theology. The spirit of freedom continues to persist among black people; consequently, black theology responds to this positive divine and human relationship. On the negative side, the polarization among different races, continued antiblack racism, and the downward turn for poor folk, especially for African Americans entangled in the web of poverty, permeate the nation. In the midst of both these signs of liberation and signs of broken community, African American churches face a life-and-death struggle. On one hand, we find a growing number of black churches catering to conservative forces in the country. They emphasize the accumulation of wealth and a prosperity gospel: preserving the status quo of elite white power, privileging the individual self at the expense of the community, and squeezing out whatever advancements possible for upper-income black people. They are seduced by and embrace the larger sinister culture of immediate gratification, the fairy-tale illusion of becoming an instant millionaire, or the never-ending quest to establish a start-up company to compete with Silicon Valley corporations. They foster a spirituality that removes the individual from this world in order to feel good in the midst of material suffering and psychological wounds, while avoiding Jesus' mandate to revolutionize systems on earth on behalf of those lacking the resources to impact the direction of the nation or their lives on a daily basis. I think feeling good is a definite goal in life. But how can one feel good as an individual when that me-focused spirituality does not make one accountable to the pain and suffering in American society?

On the other hand, we see those churches practicing black theology; they live out what the spirit of liberation calls them to say and do—to be with those who do not have a voice in society. These religious gatherings serve as a prophetic yeast for the rest of the African American community by urging people to remember the tradition of their slave ancestors, their West African forebears, the heroic role played by black churches in the civil rights movements of the 1950s through the 1970s, and the message and practice of Jesus when he walked this Earth.

Moreover, these prophetic black churches remain rooted deeply in the community outside of the church walls: offering day care, senior citizen housing, and academic and theological education. They provide preaching that uplifts people's souls but also moves their spirits to go out to change the material world as they confront groups with disproportionate privileges and harmful powers. Likewise, these faith communities participate in local and national politics, even boycotts. And they engage in a new type of missionary work to Africa and the Caribbean where political solidarity is given in opposition to U.S. imperialist policies. Furthermore, these African American churches act in a pioneering way by sharing resources and inviting local African churches to utilize these offerings as they see fit. They support the formal education of a new generation of preacher intellectuals by giving scholarships to progressive seminaries. Prophetic churches preaching and practicing black theology offer healing for the black family and make available therapy sessions, marital counseling and conferences, prison visitations, drug counseling, domestic violence ministries, support for lesbian and gays, and networking among professional blacks so that they can do pro bono work with working-class members of the church and broader communities. In addition to traditional black church structures—such as Bible study, economic development, prayer circles, and mentoring programs—the curricula of prophetic churches include an analysis and critique of U.S. monopoly capitalism, an understanding of black religious history starting with Africa, and support for all oppressed people occupying the underside of history.

Black theology sees no separation between the so-called secular and the sacred; the spirit of liberation reigns in all of reality.

Additionally, black theology touches the intellectual depths and emotional yearnings of white communities and all individuals, regardless of race or ethnicity, who are concerned about issues related to what it means to live responsibly in today's world. All people are searching and questioning the nature of their faith in the present-day commodified and consumerist culture—a fast-paced, get-rich-quick, you-can-have-it-now, superficial culture. Although we emerge from unique cultural backgrounds, we all face similar issues: Who are we and how are we related to our neighbor? What do we do in relationship to our families? What does the future hold in our turbulent times of pain and struggle, sadness, and joy?

Essentially, black theology grapples deeply and sincerely with the human questions of today. And, with much passion, it searches for definite answers to these challenges because many of those questions in the United States are exacerbated when they pertain to the African American community. And so the emotional passion, intellectual clarity, and life-and-death sense that there is something at stake characterizes the contributions and longevity of black theology. When whites, thirsting for a new way to be human, encounter these questions and answers and discover that they are addressed with heart and head, they have the opportunity to open themselves to the reality of humane and just living with blacks and with all brown, red, and yellow people. In our mutual humanity, based on commitment to the freedom of poor folk, we all thirst for some safe and comforting space where we can open ourselves to intellectual interrogation of our existential feelings. Black theology achieves precisely that; it brings together pain and pleasure, sacred and secular, and heart and head.

A black theology of liberation reminds everyone continually of the necessity of experiencing a passionate love for people, especially those without voices. To love another is to recognize oneself in the face and life of another. To love someone is to immerse and expose oneself in the context and conversation and culture of another. Love is the ultimate risk of faith—a faith grounded in liberation of all humanity; a faith with a vision for a new heaven and a new earth where each person can achieve the fullest realization of her or his calling as it serves the greater collective whole. To have such a love is to have a hope that springs from within and from on high.

Through the ups and downs and apparent lack of progress, what is it that sustains us? Even when it looks like all the world is going to hell, this hope can carry a people through. Faith, hope, and love embody a black theology of liberation. But more than that, they are what continue to keep poor and marginalized folk alive and seeking a better life for themselves, their children, and their grandchildren.

From my parents' life and the formal mentoring of James H. Cone, I learned that a theology of liberation without the heart is callous intellectual generality. And a theology of liberation without the head is mindless, empty emotionalism. I want my children, and their children, and this new generation to realize that to be free, we need the strengths of both heart and head—that is, the spirit of liberation theology from the black perspective.

LIBERATION OF THE LEAST

In the Book of Matthew (25:31-46), an instructive story offers concise insight into the decisive dimensions of a healthy society. Jesus underscores how true compassion and an authentic humanity are defined by people's relationship to "the least" among them. The least include the hungry, the thirsty, the stranger, the homeless, the naked, the sick, and the prisoner. None of these marginalized sections of society owns any wealth or occupies a high rank in the public. They lack a voice and are located at the bottom of the population. Yet Jesus emphasized that the future new, human community on earth depends on elevating the least. To work toward this ultimate goal is the sole purpose of all humanity.

Likewise Jesus elaborates one purpose for his own ministry—liberation of the least. His mission becomes clear in the Book of Luke (4:18-21) where the sacred spirit gives Jesus a vocation concentrated on the poor, the imprisoned, the sick, and the oppressed groups. Again, we see a sacred focus on the liberation of the least to reach their fullest possible human potential and to share equally in the earth's wealth. The final outcome of liberation is to practice freedom—freedom for each person to pursue his or her strengths as he or she serves the collective humanity with all the resources that the earth and technology can offer.

Heart and Head presents a variety of chapters and challenges for the twenty-first century. It draws on the rich fountainhead of African American experiences and offers them as lessons for a healthy human community. A persistent accent in black Americans' life and history is lifting the least out of a social structure that locks out a large proportion of black people from positive positions of power, privilege, and prestige while forcing them into the highest instances of a negative lifestyle in the country. This demonic economic and political structure uses race to segregate most African Americans away from too many human and civil rights that the majority population regularly expects as its God-given entitlement. In this sense, the powerful of this system portray black folk as pathological people. Still, the fact that a small group of families in the United States privately owns and controls the majority of the wealth (i.e., the land, industries, major civic and educational institutions, technology, and so forth) opens up encouraging and creative possibilities for all the oppressed pursuing a common goal. Everyone exists in the same boat. If the leaks of injustice persist, then the whole boat sinks to its ruin.

With the stories of Jesus and the progressive traditions within African American communities, privileged people can define their humanity by improving the oppressed's humanity. As if they were responding to a sacred vocation—a calling—the more fortunate share their privileges and risk sacrifices for the poor neighbor. In fact, *Heart and Head* offers the basic theme of liberation of the poor as a crucial path toward healing the brokenness and transforming injustices found in America and the world.

This book presents *black theology of liberation of the poor* as a vision and a way of life. A *black theology* grows out of the best that African American communities of faith have to offer. Those traditions emphasize right relations among people based on advancing the standard of living of and access to opportunities for the least among all of our neighbors. *Liberation* emerges from the parables and lessons of the Jesus story that call out the sacred parts of the human condition—the longing for community by judging life not by the ups and downs of Wall Street but by the well-being of the most broken and vulnerable among the citizenry. The *poor* indicates first the material poor; those who own or control no wealth. For instance, if two people work at a job and they both earn $20,000 a year, it would seem that they are equal. But what if one of the persons owns an oil field in Colorado or Texas? Let's say that both people are fired from their job and lose their income of $20,000. Both people will not suffer equally. Why? Because the one who owns and controls the oil field still has wealth. Wealth is the ownership and control of the earth's resources—the products that come from the earth and the technology that is based on scientific experiments. According to one's connection to wealth (and not income), most Americans are working people, the working poor, or in poverty. A black theology of liberation believes that there is something sacred when all of humanity share equally in all available resources and opportunities on earth. Ultimately it is a question of a spiritual view of community where each individual has a positive sense of self in the process of building common wealth for all.

PART ONE

DEFINING BLACK THEOLOGY FOR THE TWENTY-FIRST CENTURY

CHAPTER ONE

Black Theology of Liberation and the Impact of Womanist Theology

Black theology of liberation means thinking about how the spirit of liberation works with poor black folk spiritually and materially, individually and collectively, and privately and publicly. The foundation for black theology has always existed whenever and wherever God has chosen to colabor with the poor for justice. Moreover, black theology analyzes specific events and times when God gives communities at the bottom of society the freedom to choose life when they live as full human beings. And black theology presupposes that working people and the poor possess an active faith that inspires them to practice freedom as a major definition of what it means to be a full human being. In the last analysis, there exists a hope among justice-minded people that the disproportionate amount of white power on earth and the suffering of oppressed people represent finite phases on the journey toward a healthy and healed human community. Another way of putting this is: Storm clouds might gather at the midnight hour, but joy comes in the morning.

Black theology started mainly with Christian pastors, who were convinced that God's gift of liberation was present both inside and outside of the African American church. In fact, they believed that the revelation of God's love for the least in every society had no institutional boundaries.

To construct their contemporary statements on the God–human efforts for human freedom, the founders of black theology drew on a long tradition in black religion in North America. The major model came from the slavery period. Nat Turner, a Baptist preacher, heard voices from the spirit of liberation that led him to use Christianity for insurrection against the slave system in Virginia in the year 1831. Harriet Tubman left enslavement on a Maryland plantation and walked to freedom in the North. But the spirit of liberation compelled her to return many times to the enslaved South in order to free other slaves. Because of these successful secret acts, she is hailed as the Moses of the Underground Railroad (that is, the clandestine paths from the slave South to the North and Canada). In the nineteenth century, the African Methodist Episcopal Church bishop Henry McNeil Turner proclaimed that God was a Negro. And in 1923, Marcus Garvey built a six-million-member organization in his Universal Negro Improvement Association and preached that God and the Madonna were both black.

Contemporary black theology began with the formation of the ad hoc National Committee of Negro Churchmen (NCNC) in the summer of 1966, specifically with the publication of their "Black Power Statement" in the *New York Times* (July 31, 1966). A month earlier, in June of 1966, the black power challenge was issued from black students in the civil rights movement. For African American Christians, the question was immediate and clear: Is it possible to be black and Christian? Could the gospel of Jesus Christ affirm that black people should possess power as well as a strong sense of their cultural roots?

This first stage of black theology included primarily radical black clergy who were connected to churches and community movements for justice. They also debated theological issues with their white counterparts and mapped out aspects of a beginning black theology. In the specific context of Christianity, the NCNC stated that black power and black consciousness revealed the presence of Jesus Christ the Liberator. Furthermore, they analyzed how the essence of Christianity was deliverance of and freedom for the oppressed on earth.

The formation of the NCNC in 1966 marked stage 1 of black theology, in which African American clergy, administrators, and educators attempted to separate the theological reflection and practice of black religion from that of the conservative and liberal theologies of the white churches. Black theology began as a criticism both of white conservative theology's rejection of the role of the black church in the civil rights movement and of white liberal theology's denial of the relation between black religion and black power. Black theology put forth liberation of the oppressed as the key thread throughout the Christian gospel. For the creators of contemporary black theology, the good news of Jesus Christ was not neutral; Christianity concerned power—those with it and those without.

Stage 2 of black theology began in 1970, with the creation of the Society for the Study of Black Religion. Black theology became an academic discipline in graduate schools, where black religious scholars emphasized religious issues among themselves. By this time, more African American professors had been allowed into divinity schools and seminaries. They struggled over issues such as the relation between liberation and reconciliation, God's goodness and human suffering, African religion and black theology, and the spontaneous faith expressions of African American people versus the theological systems of white graduate schools.

More discussion took place about the non-Christian examples and movements that also represented black theology. In brief, God's liberation for the least in society showed itself through Jesus the Christ (for Christians). But this same spirit also appeared wherever liberation took place for oppressed people suffering internal, spiritual pain and external, structural exploitation. Although black theology turned more toward an academic emphasis in this phase, various historic black church hierarchies also began to respond favorably to different doctrines of the theology.

Stage 3, in the mid-1970s, gave birth to a new organization called the Black Theology Project (1975)—made up of church persons, community activists, and scholars—with a strong connection between African Americans and the Third World. The broad range of participants in this new group reflected black theology's turn toward liberation theologies in the Third World and a brief look at forms of African socialism, the day-to-day survival issues in the black community, black theology's relation to the African American church, and the importance of feminism and Marxism.

The fourth and current stage started in the early 1980s when the first generation began to produce doctoral students. This period includes new voices concerned with both Christian and non-Christian aspects of black life, especially African indigenous religions, modified African religious practices in the Caribbean and Latin America, black Islam, and most strikingly, the cutting-edge challenge of womanists. These black female religious scholars have pressed for a holistic black theology that integrates race, class, gender, sexual orientation, and ecological analyses. Womanists also have shown the necessity of doing black theology from such innovative sources as African American fiction and women's roles in the Bible. Furthermore, this fourth stage is marked by more pastors and professors studying and preaching black theology.

THE CONSEQUENCES OF BLACK THEOLOGY

Method in theology responds to the question: How do people arrive at answers in their talk about and practice with God among the poor? How do they come to conclusions about relations among God, humanity, and the world? What sources are their starting point; what are their normative presuppositions; and what are the consequences of their theology? As a liberation theology, black theology is a systematic and constructive movement arising from the reality of God's emancipating power that exists in all parts of life. God is present in all sources or aspects of black existence, especially that of the poor.

The Bible presents an abundance of stories about human tribulations and triumphs. These sacred tales enrich immensely black theology's creativity. Today's poor African Americans have a parallel message of oppressed conditions and struggle for freedom to that of stories in the Hebrew and Christian scriptures. The Hebrew scriptures reveal Yahweh compassionately hearing and seeing the dire difficulties faced and experienced by the bottom of society, in this case, the Hebrew slaves. When people living in a system of poverty today read the story of enslaved Hebrew workers and their relationship to a liberator God, they can see that they are not alone in their cruel predicament in contemporary America.

The exodus story offers a picture of a similar people who suffered at the hands of brutal taskmasters; were accused falsely; were pursued by forces of prejudice; suffered through a wilderness experience; went through periods of anxiety, fear, and doubt about the future; at times longed for a return to their former status in an inhuman system; argued with their leaders; and yet doggedly pursued the way to freedom.

Moreover, the African American poor, reading the Hebrew scriptures from their location on the underside of American society, discover a whole new world different from the dominating Christianity and theology of mainstream American believers. The exodus story does not end with harsh difficulties. On the contrary, the hope of deliverance cancels out the pain and energizes today's poor to keep on keeping on. The certainty of victory, witnessed in the Hebrew scriptures, empowers the poor in the midst of their deepest self-doubt.

Likewise, the black poor bring their own life issues to the stories in the Christian scriptures. And Jesus meets and greets them as their liberator, the one who can perform miracles—turning the impossible into the possible. The lowly birth of Jesus, his singular purpose to be with, struggle with, and set free the oppressed; his constant harassment by the official authorities who questioned his claims to usher in a new society for the least in his day; his eventual death sanctioned by government officials and the police; and his final triumph of resurrection all bring hope, a sense of possibilities, and power for the poor. And so the first source of black theology is the relationship between the positive promise of justice and freedom found in the Bible, on one hand, and a similar thirsting for a new way of believing and living experienced by African American poor people today.

For black theology, the black church brings together the believers in the biblical stories of spiritual and material freedom. The African American church is still the most organized institution controlled solely by black people. It is made up predominantly of poor and working people, of which up to 70 percent are women. Its class and gender composition provides a fertile basis for the development, construction, and implementation of a black theology of liberation, because African American women are usually at the bottom of American society and the black church is often located in the heart of the black community. Its vibrant and holy worship experience enables its members to renew their spiritual and emotional strength into forms of self-respect and "somebodyness," vital ingredients for survival and protracted self-development.

Its language and rhythm of preaching, praying, and testifying empower the cultural aspects of black life, thus validating that black English, call-and-response rituals (or talking back to the preacher), and black folk's ways of thinking are worthy and authentic. Its economic resources and other forms of wealth (buildings, publishing centers, transportation vehicles, auditoriums, dining facilities, credit unions) on a national scale could offer an independent financial base for an alternative way of witnessing in a society that continually makes black life and labor expendable.

Following the church and the Bible, a faith tradition of struggle for liberation makes up the third area from which to develop a black theology. Of course, the black church contains within its heritage a strong history of justice preaching and practice, starting from the indigenous religions of the first Africans forced to the "New World," through the invisible institution of slave religion, until today when liberating Christianity can be found in some local African American churches. At the same time, a faith tradition of struggle has existed outside formal church structures, most notably in the various periods of justice work of black civic, cultural, student, women's, and political organizations. God has offered the grace of freedom wherever God has chosen to freely give freedom. The possibilities of a liberated life extend beyond institutional religion.

African American women's experience constitutes the fourth source. If black women are the overwhelming majority of black church members and over half of the African American community, then black theology must speak to and reflect the intellectual and emotional concerns and contributions of women. A black theology without African American women would not be a complete and real theology. Indeed, black theology would be hypocritical if it claimed that God was for the liberation of all people yet supported only the minority male issues within the community and church.

Finally, black theology draws on the endless well of black culture— art, literature, music, folktales, black English, and rhythm. Liberation motifs in nonexplicit Christian stories have always been with African Americans. One thing, among many, that crossed the Atlantic Ocean from the west coast of Africa to American slave colonies was the heroic and unending efforts of Anansi the spider, passed on through storytelling. Anansi the spider signifies the small and disempowered being able to outsmart those with power and survive. Jazz, too, periodically served as a creative and unique form of protest, refusing to fit within the stiff styles and linear themes of European and Euro-American music. Black people's unique approach to sports, including a celebratory and in-your-face flair, has exhibited a declaration of "I am somebody" in a world controlled by others of a different class and color. The extended family, arguably another art form, provided a way of life of survival and maintenance but also became a place to groom and affirm the minds of the young who could possibly one day become another Harriet Tubman, Sojourner Truth, Martin King, or Malcolm X. Liberation culture is vital for a constructive black theology.

Yet, what is it that interweaves throughout any source of black theology that makes this form of God-talk and God-walk liberation? It is the presence of the spirit of liberation itself that gives life to and judges the usefulness of each source. The theologian holds up this spirit as the yardstick to measure all the sources and asks: Where can examples of liberation be found in these sources?

Method not only includes sources from black experiences and the yardstick of liberation but also the rhythm of doing black theology, which starts from a prior commitment to and encounter with the poor in the African American community. From a social location within the black poor, theology then moves to working in solidarity with all poor people. How faith is practiced defines the first part of the rhythm. Because the spirit of comfort, hope, and liberation already exists among the marginalized in society even before the theologian works with them, the theologian has to get involved with this life-giving movement between the poor and a liberating spirit.

From a relationship with the poor and their concerns, theology develops as a second step within the rhythm of black theology. Theology, in fact, is systematic, self-critical, and constructive thinking about the practice and faith of liberation of grassroots people within and outside of the church.

The third dimension of black theology's methodological rhythm is the return of theology back to the practice of faith to further the pastoral, ethical, political, cultural, economic, linguistic, and everyday way of life of the black poor trying "to make a way out of no way" with their liberator God. And the rhythm continues. We start with the practice of faith, move toward thinking about theology, and return to the practice of faith. The key at each moment is whether the spirit of freedom is present or not.

WOMANIST THEOLOGY

One of the most important and innovative creations in the method of black theology is the emergence of womanist theology. Womanist theology started within black theology. Now it is its own faith practice and academic discipline. The roots of this theological process go back to the middle and late 1970s, when black female graduate students at Union Theological Seminary in New York began to raise questions about the silencing or oppression of women in African American churches and in black theology.

Womanist theology is the term chosen by black female religious scholars, pastors, and laywomen who wish to name and claim two things: (1) the positive experiences of African American women as a basis for doing theology and ethics and (2) the separation of black women from both the racism of white feminist theologians and the sexism of black male theologians. Womanist theology evolves out of black theology and therefore has separate theological beliefs from white feminist theology, which ignores racism. In this way, womanist theologians join with their black brothers in the struggle against white supremacy in the church, the society, and the academy. The experience of being black in America unites womanist and black theologies.

At the same time, their female gender experience in patriarchal America lays a basis for black women's coalition with white feminists. African American female religious scholars have to live out their dual status of race and gender before God. Womanist theology affirms the unique connection between God and black women and must struggle against white supremacy and black patriarchy.

Womanist theology, moreover, takes its theological guidelines from the definition of *womanist* given by Alice Walker in her book *In Search of Our Mothers' Gardens: Womanist Prose.*

> Womanist 1. From womanish. (Opp. of "girlish," i.e., frivolous, irresponsible, not serious.) A black feminist or feminist of color. From the black folk expression of mothers to female children, "You acting womanish," i.e., like a woman. Usually referring to outrageous, audacious, courageous or willful behavior. Wanting to know more and in greater depth than is considered "good" for one. Interested in grown-up doings. Acting grown up. Being grown up. Interchangeable

with another black folk expression: "You trying to be grown." Responsible. In charge. Serious.

2. Also: A woman who loves other women, sexually and/or nonsexually. Appreciates and prefers women's culture, women's emotional flexibility (values tears as natural counterbalance of laughter), and women's strength. Sometimes loves individual men, sexually and/or nonsexually. Committed to the survival and wholeness of entire people, male and female. Not a separatist, except periodically, for health. Traditionally universalist, as in: "Mama, why are we brown, pink, and yellow, and our cousins are white, beige, and black?" Ans.: "Well, you know the colored race is just like a flower garden, with every color flower represented." Traditionally capable, as in: "Mama, I'm walking to Canada and I'm taking you and a bunch of other slaves with me." Reply: "It wouldn't be the first time."

3. Loves music. Loves the moon. Loves the Spirit. Loves love and food and roundness. Loves struggle. Loves the Folk. Loves herself. Regardless.

4. Womanist is to feminist as purple to lavender.[1]

Walker's four-part definition embodies aspects of tradition, community, self, and a critique of white feminism.

WOMANIST HISTORY

Womanist theology has a history that grows out of both the 1970s white feminist movement and the 1950s and 1960s black civil rights and black power movements. As the civil rights struggle picked up momentum and limited victories, white feminists began to push more strongly for the passage of the Equal Rights Amendment in the late 1960s and 1970s. The results of the feminist movement, from the perspective of womanists, meant at least two things: the increased presence of white women in various jobs and in seminaries and the realization by black women that racism still persisted in the feminist movement. Although black women were obviously female, they still experienced racial hierarchy in their jobs and professions with white women.

Similarly, in the 1950s civil rights and 1960s black power movements, African American women faced patriarchy from African American men. The classic story describes a meeting between Stokely Carmichael, then chair of the Student Nonviolent Coordinating Committee (SNCC), and some of its black women members during the late 1960s. In this conversation the black women raised questions about the fair treatment and recognition of women in the organization; Carmichael's response was that the only position for black women in the movement was a "prone" position. It is precisely this type of oppressive attitude and exploitative practice that black men carried into seminaries. Just as white women were increasing their numbers in graduate schools of religion, so were black men. When African American women slowly began to enter seminaries, they were faced by African American men's resistance to their receiving ordination and by a denial of black women's calling by God.

The phrase *womanist theology* was created several years after a 1979 article that hinted at a need for a black feminist theology. Written by Jacqueline Grant and titled "Black Theology and the Black Woman," the article called into question the most fundamental belief of black theology as a theology of liberation. It challenged African American men's apparent overconfidence in liberation by illustrating how black theology contradicted its own criteria. Specifically, Grant argued that if black theology described itself as a theology of liberation—meaning that Jesus Christ was with the most oppressed and God was working for the liberation of the least in society—then why was it that black theology, at best, was silent about African American women and, at worst, oppressed black women? The point was clear: Black theology cannot claim to be for justice and simultaneously treat black women as second-class citizens. In this article, Grant also drew lines of theological demarcation with white feminist theologians, but she emphasized that her primary focus was the development of an African American woman's voice in black theology.

Grant concluded that black women are invisible in black theology. She observed that two derogatory justifications pervaded the classroom: (1) African American women have no place in the study of God-talk and God-walk, and (2) black men are capable of speaking for black women. Similar conclusions can be drawn about black women in the African American church and the larger society. Grant wrote the following criticism of black religious institutions:

> If the liberation of women is not proclaimed, the church's proclamation cannot be about divine liberation. If the church does not share in the liberation struggle of black women, its liberation struggle is not authentic. If women are oppressed, the church cannot be "a visible manifestation that the gospel is a reality."[2]

The very first written work to use the term *womanist* was Katie Cannon's 1985 article "The Emergence of Black Feminist Consciousness." Championing Alice Walker's concept of "black womanist consciousness," Cannon observed that black feminist consciousness may, in fact, be more accurately defined as black *womanist* consciousness. Cannon writes that the black womanist tradition

> provides the incentive to chip away at oppressive structures, bit by bit. It identifies those texts that help Black womanists to celebrate and to

rename the innumerable incidents of unpredictability in empowering ways. The Black womanist identifies with those biblical characters who hold on to life in the face of formidable oppression. Often compelled to act or to refrain from acting in accordance with the powers and principalities of the external world, Black womanists search the Scriptures to learn how to dispel the threat of death in order to seize the present life.[3]

Cannon's scholarship introduced womanism as the innovative and new description for all black women's religious work; however, the first written text using the specific phrase *womanist theology* was by Delores Williams. In "Womanist Theology: Black Women's Voices," which appeared in the March 2, 1987, edition of *Christianity & Crisis*, Williams used Alice Walker's definition of womanism as a theoretical framework for black women's theology.

Summing up the quilt-like quality of womanist diversity in harmony and solidarity, Linda E. Thomas writes the following about the complementary threads and rainbow strands in womanist theology:

We are university, seminary and divinity school professors. We are ordained and lay women in all the Christian denominations. Some of us are full time pastors; some are both pastor and professor. We are preachers and prayer warriors. We are mothers, partners, lovers, wives, sisters, daughters, aunts, nieces and we comprise two thirds of the black church in America. We are the black church. The church would be bankrupt without us and the church would shut down without us. We are from working class as well as middle class backgrounds. We are charcoal black to high yellow women. We love our bodies; we touch our bodies; we like to be touched; we claim our created beauty. And we know that what our minds forget our bodies remember. The body is central to our being. The history of the African American ordeal of pain and pleasure is inscribed in our bodies.[4]

METHOD IN WOMANIST THEOLOGY

In the development of theology and ethics, womanists talk about an inclusive or total relation to the divine. For them, this means that African American women cannot be focused on one point. So they argue for positive sacred–human connections around issues such as gender, race, class, sexual orientation, and, to a certain degree, ecology. In fact, an inclusive method and an inclusive worldview define what it means to do womanist theology, which embraces and employs the many theological examples of oppression and liberation; many disciplines and analyses; and the diverse dimensions of what it means to be a human being—that is, the spiritual, cultural, political, economic, linguistic, and other realms.

Furthermore, in the words of Delores Williams, womanist theological method is "informed by at least four elements: (1) a multidialogical intent, (2) a liturgical intent, (3) a didactic intent, and (4) a commitment both to reason and to the validity of female imagery and metaphorical language in the construction of theological statements."[5]

Multidialogical intent allows Christian womanists to participate in many conversations with partners from various religious, political, and social communities. In these discussions, womanists focus on the "slow genocide" of poor African American women, children, and men caused by systems of exploitation. *Liturgical intent* means that black female religious scholars will develop a theology relevant to the black church, especially its worship, action, and thought. At the same time, womanist theology confronts the black church with prophetic and challenging messages coming out of womanist practices. Black church liturgy has to be defined by justice. *Didactic intent* points to the teaching moment in theology as it relates to a moral life grounded in justice, survival and quality-of-life considerations. All of these concerns can yield a language that is both rich in imagination and reason and filled with female story, metaphor, and imagery.

The method of womanist theology includes both epistemology and practice, that is, how we obtain knowledge and how we practice our ethics. How do womanists get their knowledge and how does knowledge relate to their practice? In the analysis of Kelly Brown Douglas, womanist theology is accountable to ordinary women—poor and working-class black women. This means that womanists must reach beyond the seminaries and divinity schools and go into churches and community-based organizations—this is how womanist theologians will make theology more accessible. And if womanist theology is accountable to church and community-based women, then womanist conversations must take place beyond the academy; womanist theology must have as its primary talking partners and primary location poor and working-class women and their realities in churches and community organizations. Moreover, womanist theology must work with church women to help empower them generally and to assist them in creating change vis-à-vis the church leadership. African American women comprise up to 70 percent of black churches and are the financial supporters and workers of the church.

For Linda E. Thomas, the method used by womanists "validates the past lives of enslaved African women by remembering, affirming, and glorifying their contributions." After digging up and reflecting critically on these foundational foremothers' stories, womanists then construct a new model. The new paradigm, for Thomas, includes learning from the innovative rituals and commonsense knowledge of black foremothers who overcame hostile environments.[6] Furthermore, womanist methodology uses ethnographic approaches, which allow African American women scholars to enter the actual communities of poor black women "in order to discover pieces to create a narrative for the present and the future."[7]

Summing up the holistic or inclusive dimension of the various sources in womanist theology, Emilie M. Townes states that the cornerstone of womanist belief and practice is the black church and larger community. From this environment, womanists learn from sacred and secular black writers and singers, academic conversations, black folktales, and even vodun and West African indigenous religions.[8]

One of the most creative models for practicing womanist theological method was initiated by Teresa L. Fry.[9] From 1988 to 1994, in Denver, Colorado, Fry worked with African American women in churches, individual interest groups, and various other organizations. In this model, participants ranged from 500 to 600. Fry states that the women created S.W.E.E.T. (Sisters Working Encouraging Empowering Together), which was an intentional womanist effort to support black women's spiritual and social liberation. The project was truly inclusive: ages 7 through 78; educational levels from grade school to graduate school; women who were married, widowed, single, and divorced; heterosexual, lesbian, and bisexual members; faith perspectives from ecumenical to interfaith to unchurched to personalized spiritual feelings; some who "had been incarcerated, on the way to jail or knew someone there"; and "Deltas, Alphas, Zetas, Sigmas, and Links sitting alongside Granny, MaDear, Mama, Big Momma, and Auntie."

S.W.E.E.T. organized

> annual seminars, inclusive seminars, intensive women centered Bible
> studies, monthly workshops, relationship building exercises, small
> group discussions, potluck dinners, informal and formal luncheons,

community action projects, intergenerational mentoring groups, individual and group counseling sessions, guest speakers, and in group speakers, panel discussions, role playing, ethnographies, health support groups, and African American women's literature study and discussion groups. Alice Walker's definition of womanist was used as the point of departure of each discussion . . .

The following was added to Walker's definition: a S.W.E.E.T. womanist also "believes in Somebody bigger than you and me" or "possesses a radical faith in a higher power."

Throughout the sessions, women were encouraged to think for themselves and form their own opinions and models of life by taking seriously their own experiences. In addition, each person had a chance to lead meetings. One rule governed all of S.W.E.E.T.'s activities: "We will respect our sister's space, speech, issues, voice, pain and sensitivities." Women used titles such as Sister, Girlfriend, or first names. And elders were respected with the designation of Mother (for the spiritual anchors of the group) or Miss.

Women were not pressured to be a member of a church and there was an understanding that the group was spiritually based. Each sister determined and articulated her own sense of spirituality. African American spirituality is the conscious awareness of God, self, and others in the total response to Black life and culture. It is the expressive style, mode of contemplating God, prayer life, and that which nourishes, strengthens and sustains the whole person. We coupled prayer, testimony, tears, laughter, or silence with embracing each other.

Further S.W.E.E.T. activities included interviews with members' mothers, grandmothers, and other mothers; investigations of black women leaders in different fields and in history; discussions on how to change and save the black family based on African family values; black clergy-women in the pulpit, revisioning inclusive liturgies, and seeing women's roles in the Bible; "Back to the Kitchen Table" programs held on Saturday mornings in different homes; an intergenerational group, "It Takes an Entire Village to Raise a Child"; and "Loving and Care for Yourself" gatherings—concerning hysterectomy, breast cancer, divorce, new Christians, single mothers, exercising, and self-affirmation.

So far we have looked at the origin of black theology, its stages of development, its themes, its method, and the challenge and contributions of womanist theology. However, another question needs an answer: What is the role of the church and its relation to black theology?

THE HOPE OF THE FUTURE

The main institutional hope for African American people remains the black church, which is still the oldest, most organized, most spirit-supporting community for black life and for potential radical social transformation. The church is called to witness on several different levels. On a pastoral level, the church is called to minister to the pain and brokenness of a people who are being wounded and are wounding themselves. It is called to witness as a religious institution to practice concrete ways to help the poor "to make a way out of no way." On a theological level, the church is called to witness, in its way of life, the presence of hope of a righteous God who reveals Godself through the love, hope, and liberation of Jesus the Christ. On a prophetic level, the church is called to speak truth to the powerful in America so that those who are put down by the mighty of society will know that there is a balm in Gilead that binds the broken-hearted and battered bodies of the poor.

Therefore, the most promising pockets of hope on the local level are those very few black churches and church-related institutions that preach and practice an inclusive and holistic approach to theology and Christian witness. Specifically, they get involved in all parts of black people's lives, from political organizing to baptizing new believers. These churches have carved out a prophetic ministry while impacting both the margins and the mainstreams. In a sense, they are the African American mirror of Latin America's basic Christian communities made up of peasants and workers concerned with social change and personal salvation.

The pockets of hope found in prophetic black churches serve as pointers to possibilities of social and individual transformation for African Americans affected by race, gender, and class in the United States. Each local example shows us seeds of what a full humanity could become if it blossomed. What is missing is a national coordinated theological vision, a sober analysis, a life-giving spiritual presence, and a loose network that could help to create a new reality that would situate the bottom of society at the center of the country's top priorities. This vision would include both self-help projects inside the black community as well as pressure against governments, corporate entities, and other forces in civil society charged with the well-being of those at the bottom of the nation.

Black theology must begin with the few prophetic churches, church-related institutions, and others who are struggling to offer leadership in African American communities and who take seriously a vocational calling to empower poor and other victims of dehumanizing structures. Black churches can play an important role because they make up perhaps the only national organization owned by the African American community.

Black theologians could provide a visionary framework to aid national conversations and grassroots mobilization. At a minimum, black theology could serve to challenge all national political, cultural, and economic debate to be grounded in structural and personal transformation. Such a vision would show the profound ethical dimension of servanthood and prophesy found in the birth, life, death, and resurrection of Jesus. In addition, part of this visionary framework today is to link issues of local concern with international developments. For instance, one of the key challenges for black theology is to understand adequately the negative effects of U.S. monopoly capitalism on African American poor and working-poor communities. Faith and practice based on liberation theology must include the need for freedom from the oppressive control of global capital. Because the black church and black theologians of liberation are concerned about the total well-being of the African American community, with an accent on the poor and the working class, globalization and domestic interrelations are crucial for the doing of theology and advancing toward Christ's calling for all of us to reach expectations of our wholesome dreams and creative imaginations.

Ultimately, for black theology, the vision is to become healthy human beings for which God has called women and men to struggle. It is a vision of both a new heaven and a new earth, a building of free spaces and peaceful times. Economically, the realized vision functions on communalism because all of creation is a gift from God to all of humanity. In the beginning it was that way. A theological communalism means all people own and control God's creation equally. Wealth belongs to God, and we humans are only stewards. But the sin of human political economy has allowed a small group of families on earth to monopolize the wealth—including control, distribution, and commodity consumption—at the expense of the overwhelming majority of the global population. The fact that monopolization of wealth exists does not testify to a God-given status or even a natural ability. Monopolization of monies, capital, and resources is a human-created fact; therefore, human beings also can bring about communalism.

Politically, the new vision means democracy—a new democracy in contrast to the old style. Decision making begins with the voices and priorities of the majority of earth, the vulnerable and the marginalized. Similarly, the ideal is to have the majority of elected representatives coming from these parts of society. A key element in real majority rule will be the easy ability to recall officials whose interests become antidemocratic. Fundamentally, politics is the unleashing of the constructive wisdom given by God to poor and working-class people.

Equality is a third aspect within the full humanity vision. To be equal is to be self-critical and self-judging based on what others, those different from ourselves, have or do not have. To be equal is to ask ourselves if all citizens have similar material possessions and possibilities. Equality is essential because the nature of our humanity depends on defining and creating a society in which all have opportunities to share in abundant natural resources and accumulated technologies. No one is fully human if another has access blocked or is less than someone else in a community. Basically, to be equal is to help bring about the realization of other people's gifts that God has granted.

The vision of the new human being (female and male) and the new social relations (equal ownership of resources) comes from an empowering spirituality that produces communal interactions and creative individuality, not individualism. All values that maintain a way of life and lifestyle of "I am because we are" and "I exist to share with the community" will cover the new earth. Rather than "I think therefore I am" or "I have the right to make money therefore I am," we assume that God's creative intent is to have balance and harmony in society. A rhythm of being in the world means a proper interplay between each person achieving full capabilities and the entire society benefiting.

Whenever the neighbor suffers, then balance and harmony have been broken and damaged. The sins of human disorder, at that point, go against God's providential order.

Those in the new social rearrangement will respect and reaffirm the particularity of each people's cultural identity. Specifically, a vision of a full humanity will accent the best in the African self, for God created blackness as a grace of beauty.

CHAPTER TWO

The Preferential Option for the Poor and the Oppressed

In the context of the United States of America, the phrase "preferential option for the poor" received widespread and controversial exposure when U.S. Roman Catholic bishops published their pastoral letter "Economic Justice for All" in 1984. The preferential option for the poor is needed today more than ever. It means that those with power and privilege prefer to choose service for the poor in society. It summons the deepest sense of humanity in Christians and others who still experience profound compassion for fellow citizens tossed to the wayside in a North American marketplace operating on a hyperdrive of me-firstism and an increased concentration of the nation's wealth and resources. To prefer a specific option for working people and growing communities sinking into a system of poverty puts love of neighbor above private accumulation of things. It cuts against the grain of everything that instantaneous gratification and a commodified, consumer economy demand. In the global arena, with the United States representing the sole international superpower, we might conclude that to resist the seduction of the "American way of life" appears futile. But the preferential option for the poor serves as a spiritual calling to redefine our humanity based not on our individual possessions but on serving people who struggle to attain basic material and spiritual possessions. More specifically, the humanity of the privileged elite at the top of society arises from a recognition of the humanity of the vast nonwealthy group at the bottom of society.

Today the poor live within the context of postmodernity. Postmodernity emphasizes the lack of foundations in life, the lack of absolute justice, and the lack of clarity on right and wrong. It opposes any universal truth or total descriptions of reality. From the 1950s until today, it remains an important perspective on culture, politics, and economics. Indeed, postmodernity's move away from justice intensifies the need for the preferential option for the poor. Unfortunately, some interpretations of the implications of postmodernity have tended to obscure this fact. In contrast to these mistaken opinions, the demand for the preferential option for the poor must become the central message in postmodernity. God prefers the poor because God opposes all forms of injustice that block the full humanity of the least in society. To prefer the poor is to call for a transformed individual self in service to the larger collective ownership of all of God's creation. As colaborers with God in the struggle to realize the preferential option for the poor, we will begin to bring about the new self and the new common wealth.

Postmodernity has raised numerous issues: the lack of a singular way of analyzing reality; the fall of grand narratives about human progress; the demise of the Union of Soviet Socialist Republics; the turn toward capitalism in the People's Republic of China; the transition from smoke-stack industrial monopoly capitalist economies to information-technology and service-based economies; the transformation of the clear existence of class formations into loosely formed social strata; the decline of mainline Protestant churches and the rapid expansion of fundamentalist and evangelical churches; the introduction of such terms as "political correctness" and "multiculturalism" that obscure white supremacy and the changing of power dynamics among unequal social relations; the move from one focus to many sites of oppression and resistance; the celebration of particularity over universality; the fragmentation of voices in contrast to a single voice of protest; and the apparent change from seizing state power to integrating into existing political and economic structures.

Moreover, postmodernity suggests an endless play of language; the lack of a telos (i.e., an inevitable end where justice prevails); the call for fun and frivolity; an end to any struggle against the ruling classes; the absence of any foundation for objectivity and thus the importance of relativism (i.e., everyone is right and no one is wrong); the irrelevance of content (i.e., the rise of the persuasiveness of the medium and not the message); the change from producing useful commodities to marketing products that sell images and status; the decline of the nation-state as a result of the globalization of capital; the internationalization of monopoly capitalism's division of labor; an accent on consumption rather than on production; the denial of the possibility of art and language reflecting or representing objective beauty or truth; the emphasis on imitations or copies over the originals; and the move of former radicals, progressives, and liberals to the political center and right of center.

Given these issues about today's changes in geography, politics, race, political economy, culture, and the human condition, shouldn't we abandon the idea of a "preferential option for the poor"? Isn't this phrase an outdated longing of middle-age academics for the high times of the 1960s? Haven't today's special interest groups canceled out the reality of a sector of society called *the poor?* To respond to these questions, we need to understand what the preferential option for the poor has meant, and still means.

Although the exact phrase preferential option for the poor may be from the twentieth century, the concept is strongly rooted in the biblical tradition. The Bible uses very specific language for persons in poverty: the beggar, the weak one, the frail one, rural workers, the bent-over one, the humiliated one, the wretched, the one lacking the means to subsist, and the one humble before God. Many passages in the Bible tell us that the poor are made poor by the wicked. Amos 2:6-7 reveals that perpetrators sell "the innocent for silver and the destitute for a pair of shoes. They grind the heads of the poor into the earth and thrust the humble out of their way." People are poor because they are victims of others. Wicked people "make unjust laws," says Isaiah in 10:1-2. And they "publish burdensome decrees, depriving the poor of justice, robbing the weakest of my people of their rights, despoiling the widow and plundering the orphan."[1]

The biblical stories not only clearly define poverty as the result of human sin; they call on the human community to oppose poverty. Throughout all the messages of the prophets, we discover the recurring word against those who would trample over and exploit the least in society. Hosea, Micah, Jeremiah, Amos, and Ezekiel—and the gospel of Luke and the letter of James—clearly denounce those who create poverty and take advantage of the poor. In the Hebrew scriptures, the main message about the God–human relation is when Yahweh chooses not to favor the rich and the ruling classes of ancient times. Instead, Yahweh makes a deliberate and calculated move to hear the cries of slaves, the poor, and working people. Yahweh colabors with them to remove them from systemic oppression into liberation—a place where they can be full human beings.

In the Christian scriptures, Jesus gives us two major texts. The first is in Luke 4:18ff. Here, from the Christian perspective, it is no accident that

Jesus is handed Isaiah 61 to read. In this major public proclamation, Jesus describes how the divine spirit has anointed him to side with the poor, the imprisoned, and the broken-hearted, and to proclaim the year of the Lord or the year of Jubilee for the poor. Similarly in Matthew 25:31ff., Jesus provides explicit criteria for those who have done his work. The tests include helping the poor, the hungry, the thirsty, the homeless, and the marginalized in society. This is the only place in the Bible where clear criteria are given for those on Earth who want to eventually enter heaven. Unfortunately, according to the dominant mainstream Christian denominations, these two passages are simply spiritual stories that should not be read literally. Or the denominations claim that Jesus is using metaphors or symbols. Those who control and benefit from economic and political structures always reward those who oppose attempts to make the poor's liberation a concrete, earthly spiritual formation. But God is concerned about the concrete identities and social locations of the poor. Divine spirit shows itself in the incarnation—in the flesh of the poor. Was this not exactly who Jesus was?

This preferential option for the poor in the Bible can also be seen in the tradition of black sacred life in the United States. The poor must be treated preferentially for two reasons: because of the biblical call to do so and because of the justice tradition of poor black Americans. Examples from two time periods will suffice to explain this point. The first is the sacred life experiences of enslaved African Americans. Enslaved black workers held on to their own interpretation of the Bible. They knew that these stories had a special meaning for them. For instance, they could see themselves in the tales of the Hebrew slaves who were delivered from Egyptian bondage. They identified with the three little Hebrew boys forced into a fiery furnace because black folk worked from sunup to sundown in the scorching heat of the South and in the agricultural and service industries in the slavery of the North.

If Yahweh could hear the pitiful and lowly cries of pain and suffering from the slaves in Egypt, then most definitely the same God would hear the wailing and beseeching of similar slaves in America. That is why enslaved African Americans prayed for freedom when the material world seemed to be controlled completely by white Christian slave holders. After slavery ended, a Mrs. Minnie Folkes could tell the truth about the faith of formerly enslaved blacks. She states: "In dem back days chile, meetin's was carried on jes' like we do today some whatly. Only diffe'nce is de slaves dat knowed de mos' bout de Bible would tell an' explain what God told him in a vision . . . dat dis freedom would come to pass; an' den dey prayed for dis vision to come to pass."[2]

Enslaved black workers felt that the good news of the biblical passages were not denied by the changing events of earthly existence. Regardless of how classes, communities, or people changed, one thing was certain: "God don't like ugly." That is, the constant feature of black faith is a profound belief that God does not like anyone who harms those at the bottom of society. And black workers understood this by combining their attempts of everyday survival and freedom with their interpretation of the Bible. Their conclusion is that human beings might change, but God's love for the little ones of society and God's giving of God's self for their liberation remain a constant throughout the ages. No amount of sophisticated analysis of social changes or new theological insights could alter this belief that the divine spirit is partial to working people and others suffering. God sides with the oppressed. Indeed, it is a faith tradition among the poor that gives them the preferential option in the eyes of God.

Here the preferential option combines sacred love with the practice of freedom. Love from God is not an abstract, "touchy-feely" sensation of being warm and fuzzy. Love stands for taking steps to help people get out of poverty in order that they might practice freedom—a freedom where they are just as equal in wealth ownership and power control as all others, especially being equal in all respects to those who previously held privileges and wealth over them. Former enslaved worker Henry Baker confirms this point when he explains: "We sut'only [certainly] wuz happy in dem days tuh hear dat we wuz free. . . . We served de Lawd sho nuff aftuh we wuz sot free cause we had sumpin tuh be thankful fer. . . . Ol' man Jesse Wallace wuz a preacher en he 'clared dat God luved his folks en he sent his angels down tuh set his folks free en yuh shoulder [should have] seen de shoutin'."[3] Divine love brings freedom for those who are not able to live out their God-given right to be full human beings. It is this love for freedom that empowers the black poor and gives them hope. Hope is in a future place where a person can be able to be completely what God has made him or her to be. Ultimately, heaven contains this new place and new time. One Negro spiritual captures the sense of heaven as a location where there are no obstacles stopping poor black workers from fulfilling their vocation from God. In fact, heaven signifies a space, place, and time of perpetual gladness:

1. Dere's no rain to wet you.

    O yes, I want to go home,

    Want to go home.

2. Dere's no sun to burn you,—O yes, etc.,

3. Dere's no hard trials.

4. Dere's no whips a-crackin'.

5. Dere's no stormy weather.

6. No more slavery in de kingdom [heaven].

7. No evil-doers in de kingdom.

8. All is gladness in de kingdom.[4]

The preferential option for the poor is an ongoing and long-term process that culminates in heaven, where the poor are no longer kept from their true selves, which is happiness.

Drawing on this radical tradition of enslaved black folk's experience of Christianity, Martin Luther King Jr. is the second example of black sacred life that focused on the poor. King also took the liberation theme from the Bible and applied it to the structures of poverty in his day. Toward the end of his life, he concentrated on two crucial projects—the black working class strike in Memphis, Tennessee, and a nationwide campaign to bring all of the country's poor to shut down Washington, D.C. Never perceiving himself to be a politician, King focused his solidarity with the oppressed based on his Christian faith. Faith provided the guide for his social analysis. For instance, King raised serious questions about the overall political economy in the United States from the perspective of the least in society, saying "As we talk about 'Where do we go from here,' . . . we must honestly face the fact that the Movement must address itself to the question of restructuring the whole of American society. There are 40 million poor people here. And one day we must ask the question, 'Why are there 40 million poor people in America?'"[5]

The gradual shift of Martin Luther King Jr., an ordained black Baptist theologian, to an anticapitalist preacher shows us how, in the tradition of black sacred life, faith pushes a person to a class analysis. Black belief in the preferential option for the poor does not begin with a social analysis that the community then applies to its situation. On the contrary, from the perspective of the Bible and the African American heritage—in other words, from the traditions of enslaved black folk and of Martin Luther King—a community of believers follows God's preferential option for the poor into a radical political economy. In this instance, political economy includes questioning the capitalist system and the exploitation of all workers and the oppression of black folk. The preferential option for the poor means beginning with belief and pursuing social change. It is not faith seeking understanding; rather it is faith engaged in a radical redistribution of power and wealth on behalf of those whose voices aren't taken seriously in the United States.

This faith was the foundation for the first generation of black theologians in North America during the 1960s. Combining their heritage from enslaved black beliefs, the revolutionary theology of Martin Luther King, the black consciousness movement, and the freedom message in the Bible, black theologians applied the gospel of Jesus Christ to the survival and life-and-death conditions of the black poor in North America. When James H. Cone wrote the first two books on liberation theology in 1969 and 1970, African American faith moved closer to integrating a racial social framework with one confronting poverty. However, not until Cone's August 1977 lecture to the Black Theology Project of the Theology in the Americas conference did Marxist analysis become an intentional component of a racial social perspective. Cone put forth the following points to his African American audience:

> I reject dogmatic Marxism that reduces every contradiction to class analysis and thus ignores racism as a legitimate point of departure in the process of liberation. There are racist Marxists as there are racist capitalists, and we must struggle against both. But we must be careful not to reject the Marxist's social analysis simply because we do not like the vessels that the message comes in. If we do that, then it is hard to explain how we can remain Christians in view of the white vessels in which the gospel was first introduced to black people.[6]

From the black experience, to be a Christian in any time period is to practice a preferential option for the poor. Restated, a believer stands with the bottom of society and uses whatever class, racial, and gender analyses that will help bring about the conditions that lead to the full humanity of all.

But the concern with what comes before what—that is, the gospel mandate for the poor or a radical class interpretation—becomes more pressing because of some postmodernity claims today. If, from the postmodernity perspective, relativity means there is no right and wrong; social strata replace class consciousness; the lack of a long-term human purpose substitutes for an ultimate goal of liberation; particularity trumps universality; the appearance of many voices overcomes an overarching master story; and individualism cuts against the grain of obligation to a specific community, then it appears as if "class" is an outmoded term that evaporated with the fall of Eastern Europe and Chairman Mao. And if we accept this theory, then the latest or trendiest social analysis would make the preferential treatment of the poor unnecessary. The current use of the term "postmodernity" would decide whether the preferential option for the poor is needed or not needed. On the contrary, however, as long as any poor exist, God opposes poverty and calls on all of humanity to live a sacred life of preference for the poor.

At the same time, let me be clear: There is nothing in and of itself sacred about being poor. God has chosen a preferential option for the poor because God does not like poverty. The key is liberation and the practice of freedom for all human beings. In other words, justice minded people respond to the calling for full humanity for all, free from individualism and private monopolization. In this sense, this calling also challenges all persons who are poor and marginalized as well as those who are victims of various structural discriminations in society. Just because people are poor doesn't mean that they will not strive to monopolize God's resources and abuse God's people.

GUSTAVO GUTIERREZ

Perhaps no one else has been as clear and sharp in defining the preferential option for the poor than Gustavo Gutierrez, one of the world's leaders of liberation theology. With his usual point, Gutierrez offers three parts to his definition of the poor. His first insight concerns the economically poor. In his groundbreaking 1971 text, *A Theology of Liberation,* he writes, "The term poverty designates in the first place material poverty, that is, the lack of economic goods necessary for a human life worthy of the name."[7] Poverty, in this sense, involves people who do not own wealth; people who work everyday and can barely make ends meet; those who clean bathrooms and make up our beds; and workers in factories. Moreover, poverty includes the unemployed; the overworked; those permanently without jobs; those lacking health insurance; women who have to sell their bodies to feed their children; people who work double and triple shifts on one job; others who work two and three different jobs; those who were forced off of welfare and now work jobs that put them in worse positions; working-class people who drive buses, cabs, and subway trains; secretaries and administrative assistants; flight attendants; technicians; nurses; railroad workers; construction laborers; and others who labor and are underpaid. Today we still have a working class, working people, and the rise of a new category of workers found in new types of technological, service, and information industries.

The second form of poverty is *spiritual poverty.* It means, as elaborated by Gutierrez, being open to God and being willing to be used by God. Spiritual poverty focuses on a sacred spirituality and not on hoarding material wealth. Unfortunately, the dominant churches (the mainline churches), tend to believe that spiritual poverty includes those with lots of wealth and income who can both maintain their wealth and extraordinary income and still be poor in spirit. From this sinful belief and practice, those who exploit, oppress, and discriminate against others do not have to share their wealth and do not have to stop their evil ways. But they still can have a poor spirit. This false understanding of poverty is a highly spiritualized one; it is a hocus-pocus poverty that churches preach with the result of making Christianity an opium of the people. In this view, which stands contrary to Gutierrez, there really is nothing fundamentally different from a working-class family and a monopoly capitalist family since they both suffer spiritual poverty. In this interpretation, God has given all people spirits that we have all equally damaged. Jesus came for the poor in spirit, no matter what their economic situation. One person heads a household and works a double shift everyday. Another person heads a household and owns an island in the Caribbean or the Pacific Ocean. But they are both poor in spirit. However, a person cannot be open to God while giving allegiance to the private hoarding of God's resources.

After material and spiritual poverty, Gutierrez then elaborates on biblical poverty: "In the Bible poverty is a scandalous condition inimical to human dignity and therefore contrary to the will of God." One who is wretched, bent over, or weak exists in conditions of poverty. Gutierrez correctly reads the Bible differently. Jesus of the Christian scriptures is one who came to help the poor have a quality daily existence and ultimately have liberation in order to reach their highest potential.[8] Gutierrez challenges us to look at sacred writings through the eyes of the voiceless in our society. If Jesus' entire existence and the complete purpose of the resurrected Christ is to work with the oppressed in society, and if the entire story of the Hebrew scriptures tells us about Yahweh colaboring with slaves to move them out of oppressive structures in one space and time and into a new location of freedom, then surely our divine calling begins first with the poor.

Gustavo Gutierrez is one of the world's leaders of liberation theology. Yet, more important, it is his commitment to the gospel of Jesus Christ and his compassion for the poor that mark his way of being in the world. In his life, Gutierrez exemplifies this faith style by living and working with the poor in Lima, Peru. It is not theory or new theologies that change the world, it is action. In the final prophetic words of *A Theology of Liberation,* he concludes:

> We must be careful not to fall into an intellectual self-satisfaction, into a kind of triumphalism of erudite and advanced "new" visions of Christianity. . . . all the political theologies, the theologies of hope, or revolution, and of liberation, are not worth one act of genuine solidarity with exploited social classes. They are not worth one act of faith, love, and hope, committed . . . in active participation to liberate [women and men] from everything that dehumanizes [them] and prevents [them] from living according to the will of [God].[9]

There is a great deal to learn from a person like Gustavo Gutierrez. He has taught us that true Christianity begins with us sharing our humanity with those who have been made the underside of history, the wretched of the earth, and the marginalized in our communities, families, churches, and the world. Unfortunately, today's mainstream churches argue that a true Christian is one who supports the system of capitalism and all of its forms of focusing on the individual. That is why Christianity supports the economic and political system of the United States of America. Based on this interpretation of the gospel of Jesus of Nazareth, one would think that Jesus Christ was an American citizen supporting the Stars and Stripes and singing "God Bless America." Obviously, Gutierrez does not read the Bible this way.

Moreover, Gutierrez teaches us about a new way of doing theology. Here theology is reflection on a prior commitment to the poor. Instead of assuming that correct ideas fall from the sky, Gutierrez understands that talk about God arises from the poor. It comes from this social location because God is already present with the oppressed. It is, therefore, a theology from below. Not only does Gutierrez present us with a new epistemology by telling us where knowledge comes from, he also helps us to understand that true theology is a second step. With this lifestyle of service, we must first take a stand with the victims in our communities.

In contrast, the prevailing way of teaching and living out theology in the United States is to worship theological ancestors from Europe or white North American academics. Theologians, graduate students, and educated clergy refer to a certain group of European and white North American authorities. In order to be successful in graduate schools of religion, one practices "true" theology: One starts with the systems of these thinkers, explains their systems, and then occasionally attempts to apply these systems to the North American situation. In the status quo theology, one gains success by repeating the ideas from whites, primarily from Europe but also from North America. Yet theology would be richer if the rest of humanity (i.e. over 90 percent of the world's theoreticians and intellectuals from Africa, Asia, the Caribbean, Latin America, the Pacific Islands, and Third World peoples within the United States) were taken seriously as sources for understanding the relation between humans and God. Such democracy would broaden the complexity and creativity of doing theology.

Gutierrez brings theology back down to Earth, the only place where it can be. Theology comes from two Greek words—*theos,* or God, and *logos,* or human being. In mainline theology, God seems to do theology; theology is abstract, objective, universal truth. But we must remember that theology is *logos* about *theos*. In other words, human beings are doing theology, not God. Dominant theology gives the impression that the divine being talks about itself as God and, thus, does theology. On the contrary, God-talk is not God talking but human-talk *about* God. If we know that humans do theology and not God, then a whole host of questions arise: Who are these theologians doing theology? What are their class backgrounds and class interests? What are their racial identities and ethnicities? What is their gender? What are their sexual orientations? Do they support capitalism? Do they separate faith from the secular? What are they passionate about? Do they think that the United States of America is the best manifestation of what God wants human beings to do and be? How do they see the new society promised to us by Jesus?

Moreover, if we take seriously the lessons that theology is done by human beings and therefore we should look at the people doing the God-talk, we are confronted by the reality of the people who occupy positions of power in the institutions of religious studies. More specifically, why are 90 to 95 percent of the leadership positions of institutions in theological seminaries and graduate schools of religion occupied by white heterosexual men? Is it because God ordained this, or because white heterosexual men have a better intellect than others, or because they represent better the new society that Jesus lived and died for? I think not. I think this goes against the majority. The majority is constituted by brown, yellow, red, and black people and white working-class men and women. Institutions of religious studies reflect not the majority but a minority population. The challenge becomes: How do we broaden a way of life from a minority reality to a democracy?

Gutierrez ultimately teaches us that churches must take sides. Too often the dominating communities of faith in North America believe that it is not their duty to side with the poor against those who create institutions and a culture that make and keep them poor. Is not the church the ecclesia, those set apart to do the will of liberation for those who do not yet have a voice in society? It is understandable why North American churches do not seem to take a stand. Some churches do not know that not taking a stand is, in reality, actually taking a stand in a situation of conflict and injustice. Neutrality means siding with the status quo. Many churches have no idea how the unjust power dynamics on the national and international levels relate to the deepening of pain for people. For them, people have become victims due to their own effort or lack of efforts. This, of course, is the blame-the-victim syndrome. Other churches recognize that powerful families and institutions dominate this country. Yet these same churches do not dare follow the gospel of Jesus Christ for fear of losing money, members, and privileges. Still other North American churches have some social analysis and realize that one cannot be a true Christian unless one takes a stand with the least in society. But these churches usually are willing to give only charity, and not to work for systemic social justice and healing.

Gutierrez helps us to see that the new human being we are all longing for has to also have a profound transformation—a metanoia—on the spiritual level. Deep within the souls of each of us there lurk negative feelings, deep scars, and wounded children. How can we move into a new heaven and new earth when we are burdened with emotional and psychological baggage? How can we raise up the sacred goodness that God has given us if it is battling with, spending energy on, and being distracted by the evil of negative emotions and wounds? Spiritual healing must be part of the definition of liberation theology.[10] Many of the contemporary North American spirituality movements do not recognize this need to link spiritual healing with social change. Some people prefer spirituality instead of churches because they have been injured by the hypocrisy of faith communities. As a result, they seek an abstract spirituality that makes them feel good as individuals isolated from realities around them. But what type of spirituality can it be when one can feel good in one's spirit but still be a racist, a sexist, a heterosexist, or an ignorer of the poor? Spirituality should make us feel so good that we cannot stand seeing the sins of the world. The spiritual person would be so filled with the spirit that he or she would seek to change the world. Spirituality would give us new eyes to see with and new ears to hear with. We would see the standards for a healthy economy and a positive everyday existence being determined not by Wall Street but by the quality of life of those without wealth or massive incomes.

Gutierrez's work and writing teach us about the wisdom of the poor. How many of us really think that poor people, folk at the bottom of North American society, actually are the ones who produce the knowledge of this world? This is a revolutionary idea. If this were true, it would raise questions about all of the institutions of learning in this country. Why are people leaving these schools deeply in debt if the location of knowledge is outside these hallowed halls? If knowledge and wisdom begin from below, educational institutions would be organized around the real lives of people who live day to day keeping their families together. These are the scholars who clean our bathrooms, cut our grass, cook our food, work in the factories, and carry out the secretarial and administrative assistance work. What would it mean to refocus the nation's vision, resources, time, energy, and financial rewards on poor and working-class people? Our knowledge base and wisdom storehouse would be much richer than it is now.

A NEW COMMON WEALTH

Indeed, we need the preferential option for the poor today more than ever because postmodernity includes an intensification of worker exploitation, racial oppression, women's discrimination, and sexual identity exclusion.

In the current conversation about postmodernity and in the latest theoretical discussions on class, culture, and the economy, we must not forget those who are the underside of history. For justice minded people, we must stand first with the spirit of liberation as it lives with those suffering at the bottom of the nation. Being with this spirit on the underside causes us to fix our eyes on people living in structural poverty. Likewise, it forces us to begin with the oppressed in society as our starting point. Cornel West defines the contemporary crisis in the following manner:

> The exodus of stable industrial jobs from urban centers to cheaper labor markets here and abroad [among other factors] have helped erode the tax base of American cities just as the federal government has cut its supports and programs. The result is unemployment, hunger, homelessness, and sickness for millions. And a pervasive spiritual impoverishment grows. The collapse of meaning in life . . . leads to the social deracination and cultural denudement of urban dwellers, especially children. . . . The result is lives of what we might call "random nows," of fortuitous and fleeting moments preoccupied with "getting over"—with acquiring pleasure, property, and power by any means necessary. [Rage against women and among young black men] is fueled by a political atmosphere in which images, not ideas, dominate, where politicians spend more time raising money than debating issues.[11]

Today's environment reflects the intensification of a capitalist concentration of wealth and an addiction to the individual self. The ongoing mergers of monopoly capitalist corporations point to an unchecked tendency of hoarding God's gifts of creation given initially to all of humanity. For instance, the entertainment industry is divided into four major divisions:

General Electric (the biggest corporation in America), comprising the NBC network, numerous cable stations, and other properties.

[AOL] TIME WARNER, comprising [AOL], Time Warner Entertainment; Turner Broadcasting; CNN; Warner Brothers; HBO; numerous magazines such as *Time, Fortune,* and *Life;* numerous publishing houses such as Little, Brown and Time-Life; numerous other cable channels; numerous production services such as World Championship Wrestling; and other properties.

DISNEY CORPORATION/CAPITAL CITIES, comprising ABC network; several TV stations in major urban areas that together reached 25 percent of American households; numerous cable stations such as the Disney Channel, ESPN, and the Lifetime Network; numerous magazines; numerous newspapers such as the *Kansas City Star* and the *Fort Worth Star-Telegram;* numerous retail stores; sports teams; theme parks; record companies; motion picture companies; and other properties.

WESTINGHOUSE CORPORATION (one of the America's biggest defense contractors), comprising the CBS network; the CBS radio network; numerous cable stations such as TNN and the Nashville Network; satellite distribution companies; and, of course, Westinghouse's nuclear power and nuclear engineering divisions.[12]

Such an example is the tip of the iceberg of concentrated power in the United States of America.

If we are to be faithful to the practice of the preferential option for the poor, then we must take the risk of visioning what the future goal and ultimate society will look like. I think that the final end is a new beginning for all of humankind. This new time and new space is what I call the new self and the new common wealth. Traditionally it is referred to as the kingdom of God. This new heaven and new earth follow the example of Jesus, who established a type of faith and practice for others; he conducted his life not for himself or his inner circle but for the majority. He received internal strength in order to serve the larger human family. In a similar way, during the time of the new self and new common wealth, each individual will be able to achieve the fullest potential that God has created her or him to be. No longer will there be barriers to the full humanity of each person. Class exploitation, racial oppression, gender discrimination, and sexual identity exclusion will end. Likewise, the negative feelings internal to each person's body will come to an end. When low self-esteem, negative anger, depression, and other harmful psychic and spiritual wounds are done away with, each person can use the maximum positive spirituality inside of him or her to be all that God has called them to be.

However, this is not a vision for individualism that is simply a concentrated form of capitalist emphasis on "me first." On the contrary, it reflects individuality. Individuality differs from individualism; individuality calls for accountability and obligation to the community. But with individualism, a person harms the individual self when left to live, think, and be alone separate from the group. An individual makes skewed decisions and opts for narrow actions just for the self or even just for his or her family. The novel vision will require a new type of freedom where we are free to serve the collective interests. Indeed, in West African philosophy, without community, a person is less than an animal. Consequently, not only will there be a new self, there will also be a new common wealth. Theologically, God created all things equal. In particular, God gave all of the earth's wealth to be shared by all of us as stewards. No one in the new society, therefore, will have private ownership of wealth, which belongs to God. Human beings cannot own personally that which does not belong to them. In fact, the nonhuman creation is a gift from God to all. Thus the final goal, the ultimate aim, is to share in common all that God has created.

The new self and the new common wealth represent the final goal. Yahweh of the Hebrew scriptures promised this time and place to the Hebrew workers who were enslaved in Egypt. Jesus walked this earth, delivered his first public speech, and laid out the criteria for entering this new time and place. The Book of Revelations speaks about this final vision. In the folk wisdom of black believers, it describes what they mean when they say they'll meet you on the other side of the Jordan where there's no more pain or sorrow, only happiness. And Martin Luther King Jr. gave his life toward this end.

In addition, between the cutthroat reality of the now, on one hand, and the period of the ultimate goal, on the other hand, we envision an intermediate period. Here the preferential option for the poor becomes even more clear. During the in-between time, we envision the poor, the least sectors of society, and the marginalized people among us owning and controlling the wealth of this land. A true majority of society will govern. With this condition in place, issues of universal healthcare, housing, employment, vacations, recreations, education, day care, and all of the issues that ensure a positive quality of daily life for those who were suffering from poverty will become easily attainable. The sole criterion during this interim period will be how we participate in the process of eliminating the system of poverty and the host of related forms of brokenness in the human family.

It is through the majority of the country that the spirit will lead and work with human beings to bring about a universal liberation and the practice of freedom for all of humanity. The sacred vocation is to empower the poor, to work with them on their own negative spirituality, and also to participate in releasing them from structures of oppression created by the small group of monopoly owners of the world's wealth. Liberation means removal from the internal grip of psychological "demons" and the external restrictions of "sinful" systems. As a result, under the guidance of the divine, we all can aid in gradually re-creating a new personality and new social relations that will liberate even the minority population of monopolizers. A true full humanity includes us all so that to be human is to see one's humanity in the other. And it means a vocation of service to the most vulnerable. In the present moment, during the in-between time, and in the final ultimate, new divine reality, the anchor to our belief and practice is the preferential option for the poor. Upon this rock, we judge postmodernity.[13]

PART TWO

BLACK THEOLOGY AND SACRED LIFE

CHAPTER THREE

Spirituality and Transformation in Black Theology

The spirituality of black theology arises out of the experiences of social change and the traditions found in several stories—the radical calling in the Christian Bible, African American women's spirituality, and the folk faith of enslaved black workers. Just as the God of freedom incarnated God's self in the birth, life, crucifixion, and resurrection of Jesus the Liberator, so, too, God's same spirit of freedom incarnates itself among poor African Americans suffering in life-threatening situations and crying out in their struggle for a productive and complete life.

THE BIBLICAL STORY: A SUBVERSIVE SPIRITUALITY

Based on the Christian scriptures, the progressive sectors of the African American church, for whom black theology speaks, maintains a subversive faith in Jesus Christ's spirit. In particular, the Reverend Martin Luther King Jr. stands in this spiritual tradition when he paraphrases Luke 4:18 and proclaims: "Jesus said the spirit of the Lord is upon me, because he's anointed me to heal the broken-hearted, to preach the gospel to the poor, to bring deliverance to those who are in captivity and to proclaim the acceptable year of the Lord. And I must confess that the spirit of the Lord is upon me."[1]

In his biblical interpretation, King, a black Baptist preacher, stresses two aspects of black theological spirituality. The first act of Christian spirituality is not correct doctrine but service to the poor, the hungry, the homeless, the unemployed, victims of AIDS, immigrant strangers, and those without proper clothing. Christian spirituality means confronting the everyday pain and humiliation that face the faceless in society. It means commitment to and standing with those who suffer. To be compelled by the spirit, then, the black church has to root itself primarily in poor African American communities where the Lord's spirit was born and still resides. Christian spirituality greets the black church in the struggle for freedom—"the truth will set you free" (John 8:32)— of the least of these in the country. Indeed, for the spirituality of the eleven o'clock black church service on Sunday to be genuine, it has to receive God's presence in suffering and struggle in the Monday through Saturday black ghettoes of North America. It is this spirit that "will guide you into all the truth" (John 16:13).

Black theological spiritual practice fundamentally means social transformation of wicked structures and destructive systems that hold a boot to the necks of poor black people in the United States. Any talk about the spirit in the black church that leaves unjust social relations in place serves a devilish way of life that breeds monopoly capitalism, the second-class status of women, the harmful military presence of the United States abroad, and, of course, racial supremacy over African

Americans and other people of color. Following the Christian spirit's calling, Martin Luther King Jr. began to organize against evil structures. In the last year of his ministry, he declared: "The dispossessed of this nation—the poor, both white and Negro—live in a cruelly unjust society. They must organize a revolution against that injustice, not against the lives of the persons who are their fellow citizens, but against the structures through which the society is refusing to take means which have been called for, and which are at hand, to lift the load of poverty."

King named this spirituality of evil structures the capitalist system in the United States of America. This diabolical spirituality spread racism at home and imperialist war abroad. For instance, when he questioned the existence of domestic poverty, King replied: "and when you begin to ask that question, you are raising questions about the economic system, about a broader distribution of wealth." Basically, the anointing to follow Jesus led a person "to question the capitalistic economy." And for King, God's transformational spirit moved him to organize the beginning of the divine "kingdom"—specifically revealed in "democratic socialism." Thus politics—that is, the act of rearranging power relations in accordance with the spirit of freedom—helps to define the spiritual activity of a black theology of liberation.

In addition to a liberating spiritual practice, the anointing of "the spirit of the Lord" also commissions us to proclaim the good news of freedom. God's loving freedom has become our freedom because Jesus' victory over oppression has opened up a new world where everlasting life begins now (John 3:16). Freedom is the ability to perceive new possibilities for society that are more equal than the way things exist now; to think differently includes a re-visioning of social relations into justice. And freedom is the ability to forge a lifestyle to bring about this envisioned future. Individual freedom means intellectually and practically working to realize collective well-being. This spirit calls on black theology to speak to and for those who are silenced among the citizenry. It calls on black theology to recognize that the gospel of freedom for a full individual and collective life is a gift now for the African American poor and is in solidarity with the world's poor. Martin Luther King Jr. recognized the prophetic nature of speaking the truth of Christian spiritual anointing: "We are called," he proclaimed, "to speak for the weak, for the voiceless, for the victims of our nation."

The poor have to hear that Jesus' new society has won and, therefore, has made them somebody. The somebodiness that the gospel proclaims is not a mushy feel-good, self-indulgence. On the contrary, it empowers people living in poverty to practice their true spiritual identity. For the African American poor in particular, it affirms their African self-identity. Part of announcing a liberating spirituality to the black victims of society is to tell them that their African self or their black self comes from the grace of God. "Yes," shouted King, "we must stand up and say, 'I'm black and I'm beautiful,' and this self-affirmation is the black man's need, made compelling by the white man's crimes against him." Self-identity language of blackness and Africanness grips the poor and helps them to see, with new eyes, the reality and future potential of a new heaven on earth. When the harmful social systems and language structures propagated by white elites are subverted by the good news of a new kingdom or new common wealth, then poor black people will no longer feel defined exclusively by a white ruling culture. Then they can claim and name themselves in the free space created by Jesus' liberating spirit. To say who you are is part of struggling against dehumanizing labels that deny your total humanity. Culture, which I define as the act of identifying oneself in accordance with freedom, then, is an important aspect of black theology's transformative spirituality.

BLACK WOMEN'S STORY:
HOLISTIC SPIRITUALITY OF THE BLACK BODY

Christian spirituality and transformation in black theology are more clearly and readily seen in the biblical practice and proclamation of the Reverend Martin Luther King Jr. However, the spiritual basis of black theology also includes African American sources that are borderline to Christianity and, in some instances, non-Christian. The suggestive and imaginary novels of Toni Morrison overflow with examples of God's liberating spirituality pursuing diverse religious paths, thus broadening black theology into a complex encounter with the Holy. Specifically, black women add the liberating dimension of a spirituality of the body.

In Morrison's stories, poor African American women regard their natural bodies as sacred temples of self-love, normal physical-emotional expression, and gifts to God's spirit in worship. More exactly, Baby Suggs (a character in Morrison's novel *Beloved*) pastors a congregation of poor black folk out in a section of the woods which they call "the Clearing."[2] Here this unordained preacher woman calls on her "church" to love the flesh of their bodies and to give full play to their natural appetites for crying, laughter, and dance. Put differently, this Christian conjurer tells her people to lift up their spirits through their bodies in the rituals of dance, laughter, and crying as a way of relating to the divine spirit.

First, church service begins with Baby Suggs's sermon on self-love of the sacred human flesh. "'Here,'" preaches Baby Suggs, "'in this here place, we flesh; flesh that weeps, laughs; flesh that dances on bare feet in grass. Love it. Love it hard.'" Stressing a specific passion for a spiritual love of the body, Suggs preaches within a concrete and historical context of white racism, a context quite familiar to her congregation's collective memory and to their daily dehumanizing relation to whites in their lives. Continuing her spiritual sharing of the body's significance, she reminds her folk that "they" (referring to white cultural and political norms) despise poor blacks' "eyes" and "the skin on your backs"; "they" do not love black hands; and "they ain't in love with your mouth."

Instead, her congregation must love their flesh; stroke their hands and touch other black folk with them; grace their necks and support their backs; provide strong arms for their shoulders; and love their inside parts. Above all, Baby Suggs exclaims, "'Hear me now, love your heart. For this is the prize.'" The heart stands as the ultimate part of the body because God has given poor blacks the ability to love each other as well as all bodies that suffer and endure hatred. But in order to be human—to take God's grace of love, planted spiritually within each heart, and love the rest of humanity—African Americans have to go down deep in the depths of their black hearts and love the blackness of their physical being. Self-love, or coming to terms with the love of God created in human hearts, sets the context for resonating with the love of others, even feeling compassionate justice for one's enemies. Thus, the natural bodies reflect sacred temples of self-love.

In fact, the more poor folk love their bodies in the face of how television and Hollywood define them as cops, criminals, and comedians—all examples of antiblack racism—the more the black poor can extend a love to those who oppose them. Love of the black body is a revolutionary spirituality because it disrupts the sinful psychic of the poor who struggle with the "white person" inside of their mind and body. Self-hatred can become a lethal weapon against the African American poor. In fact, the mind and body, emotions and intellect go together. The community has to create radical rituals to exorcise and cast out the white norm inside of the African American self-definition of what it means to be a human being created in God's image. The black body is the key to judge those black folk who ape white looks or accept black looks. Black looks mean embracing and trumpeting the hair, nose, skin, lips, hips, and walk of African Americans. Such a self-affirmation is a form of praise to God. It says that the black body is the reflection of the spirit of the divine. The black body is not merely the flesh and blood creation of X and Y chromosomes or DNA instruction. The African American body is black; it is connected to the ultimate spirit. Consequently, to be black in the United States indicates divine goodness for those African Americans who would hold on to God's grace—the divine gift of being black. The black body flows from a spiritual vocation of self-affirmation as obedience to God.

Continuing with folk preacher and spiritual evangelist Baby Suggs, we find her church services calling on the spirit through the normal physical-emotional expressions of her congregation. With sacred authority, she summons forth the children and instructs them to laugh before their parents. And the children's bodies, which they loved, filled the trees with laughter. She then orders the men to step forward and dance before their wives and children. And "groundlife shuddered under their feet" as the trees rang with the sounds of children's laughter. Finally, she designates the women and tells them to cry, for the living and the dead. It began with clear roles for each segment of the folk, but then everything and everybody become intertwined and inter-mixed: "Women stopped crying and danced; men sat down and cried; children danced, women laughed, children cried until, exhausted and riven, all and each lay about the Clearing damp and gasping for breath. In the silence that followed, Baby Suggs, holy, offered up to them her great big heart."

In holy worship, Baby Suggs offers a transformative spirituality of the individual and communal body. Love of self, given by God's spirit of love and implanted in the heart, enables us to identify our spiritual self and thus hold on to the cultural identity of the body. This, in turn, helps us to deal with the "theys" of the world, which enables us to assert the political power of the body, even while understanding the position of our adversary. In addition, we return God's spiritual love through a demonstrative display of the body's natural activities of laughing, dancing, and crying. Baby Suggs, therefore, leads black theology down into a black spirituality of the natural body and into new places where God's call for life can be heard. This radical movement down includes a risk-taking spirituality where the individual is a human being only because of the person's contribution to changing the fundamental structures of society. Similarly, the individual, in this context of communal needs, is transformed in the spirit. And finally, and at the same time, the individual and community can grasp the spiritual pains and possibilities of those who hate us.

In Toni Morrison's novels, African American women's spirituality moves black theology into the realm of an inclusive and holistic divinity whose life-changing freedom manifests throughout the black church and community. This freedom from divine spirit invades the human body, connects with the existing divine spirit in the poor, gives life to it, and spreads to the entire gathering of the folk. Spirituality is a freedom that transforms the oppressed from an old self into a new self that appears in all types of instances and ways of life. God's power of loving the poor through justice and liberation knows no boundaries. As a result, an African American living with God opens heart and head, ears and eyes to wider resources in the total black spiritual experience. Black women's spirituality includes Christian and non-Christian thought and action. Such a connection between reflection and practice creates theology because it stands as an example of God's liberating spirit wherever God chooses to reveal God's Christian and non-Christian self. Black women's spirituality embraces the religion of the institutional church and the nonchurch. It is religious because an unrestrained divine initiative among humanity expresses itself both within the church institution and within the broader African American women's community, which links to the rest of black folk and, indeed, to all of poor humanity.

Furthermore, out of the soil of the poor black women's spirituality, black theology discovers new theological language, thought forms, metaphors, and categories. And so the liberating appearance of God's spirit in non-Christian revelations, through the body and through stories, complements the divine spiritual descent upon the decisive Christian revelation of Jesus the Christ: "The Spirit of the Lord is upon me" (Luke 4:18). The holistic nature of black women's religious experiences in fictional narrative shows us the expansive power of a God of liberation who will use everything to work with those without power in society to practice freedom. Obviously, Christianity remains the dominant expression of this revolutionary spirit of transformation. But God does not remove God's self from any sphere of the poor's reality. In fact, these tales of the divine and human connection teach us that black theology sees no separation of the so-called secular from the sacred; God's presence pervades all, and God's gift of working with the poor to practice equality reveals this process everywhere without boundaries. Crossing these boundaries requires a new way of talking about and imaging reality. Stories about African American women aid in this task of pleasure and struggle.

The Christian and non-Christian lives of poor African American women are authentic theological sources of divine transforming presence. In Morrison's novels, these creative women serve both as midwives for the divine spirit of power and as the medium through which the holy spirit offers a new way of change to them and to the world. In fact, the uniqueness of women's spiritual experience and story must be taken seriously precisely because a black theology of liberation receives and participates with an incarnational God who tabernacles with the poor. For black theology, one of the many experiences of the poor is the gender-racial-poverty reality of black women. And while we struggle against and dismantle wicked principalities and powers, we also open ourselves up to the multiple positive, creative, and spiritual laughter, tears, dance, and thinking of African American women. Women's spirituality of the body is inclusive and holistic.

SLAVE STORY: SPIRITUALITY OF THE FOLK

From 1619, when European Christians brought twenty Africans to the so-called New World, until 1865, when the end of the Civil War saw the fall of slavery in the United States, Christian slavemasters owned black workers like a master owning a dog. Yet enslaved Africans knew that God had given them a heart, a head, a body, and a soul infused with a divine spirituality of survival and liberation. Consequently, out of the heat of slavery, black folk worked with the spirit to empower themselves and thus re-create their crushed status into a life of new beings. In other words, spirituality compelled them to keep on keeping on even when their bodies broke while laboring from "can't see in the morning till can't see at night," a reference to working from dawn to dusk.

Ex-slave Cornelius Garner used the inspiration of a liberating spirituality to describe the absence of the divine presence in white slavemasters' churches. To Garner, the quiet stillness in white people's worship signified a heretical void that replaced God's word of freedom with a demonic, pro-slavery justification. In the language of the slave folk, Garner remembers:

> De churches whar we went to serve God was 'Pisipal, Catholick, Presberteriens, de same as marster's church only we was off to us selves in a little log cabin in de woods.

De preaching us got 'twont nothing much. Dat ole white preacher jest was telling us slaves to be good to our marsters. We ain't keer'd a bit 'bout dat stuff he was telling us 'cause we wanted to sing, pray, and serve God in our own way. You see, 'legion needs a little motion— specially if you gwine feel de spirret."[3]

For the enslaved black worker, serving God in your own way requires a movement of "de spirret." And so white preaching "'twont nothing much" because the spirit did not present itself. If the divinity does not visit the gathered faithful, then the will of God for freedom and a full healthy life remains a dream deferred and a promise postponed. Therefore, white Christians could preach that slaves should obey their masters because whites had never experienced the moving grace of a liberating spirituality. Slavemasters did not feel God's spirit because they blocked it with their focus on discriminating against blacks. Antiblack racism or white supremacy or the reflex that African Americans are secondary and come last in all spheres of life in the United States required a full spiritual concentration and effort on the part of white Christians. They could not serve two masters; they could either advocate white power over black life or pursue God's spirit of liberation for the poor and vulnerable in society. The sermons from white Christians that black workers received under slavery had nothing to do with the joy of the spirit.

In contrast, enslaved African Americans served God in their own way with complete vibrancy—by singing, shouting, and dancing. The movement of the bodies of slave folk imaged the joyous thanks and praise that they offered to God who daily gave them life amid rags and dirt. Black slave folk "got happy" because the Lord had brought them a mighty long way. Their physical motion and feeling of "de spirret" in worship meant that the chains of slavery could control neither their bodies or their spirits. Worship itself, then, became a space of defiance and proclamation for an unrestrained life. The spirit of freedom does not allow the poor to remain still. They have to shout, rock, sway, dance, sing, cry, moan, jump, clap, wave their hands, and talk back to the preacher because the spirit liberates them to another realm—a spiritual realm—where they get a taste of how to practice freedom. If the poor remained stationary in worship, they could not receive the transformative feeling greater than themselves that transports them to another time and space while keeping them still grounded on earth. That is why they sang: "I know I been changed. The angels in heaven done changed my name." Angels are spiritual servants of God who work on the body—the broken, bent over, and overworked bodies of the poor, both individually and collectively. Black religion of the oppressed requires motion to indicate the presence of the spirit.

Furthermore, slaves' spirit-filled motion suggests a change and transformation from the old to the new, a development from a state of decaying death to the birthing of a revitalized Jubilee. In this radical bringing forth of a liberated life for the vulnerable, the underside of history, a virtual war takes place between demonic and divine spirits. Another former slave describes this fierce combat: "There is a real heaven and hell. The hell is the devil and his angels. They are evil spirits and are ever present with us to tempt and try us. They are at war with the heavenly host and seek to dissuade those who would serve God."[4]

Again, African American bondsmen and women connected genuine service to God with battling evil spirits of oppression; slaves knew theologically that a real heaven and hell existed. And hell embodied and embedded itself in specific institutional and structural evils on earth. Therefore, that which attacked the motion-filled spirit of the poor was an ever-present evil. So our stand with the spiritual life of the oppressed compels us to serve with God's spirit of the "heavenly host." It requires specific acts of daily collective and individual warfare against systemic and personal evil. It means a joy in motion for a spiritual life specifically revealed in actual earthly struggle for liberation of the folk. Through the troubles of the day, our hard work and steadfast hope yield the beauty of a life worth living.

Spirituality and transformation, divine freedom and individual and collective change in black theology include real-life experiences of a poor and struggling African American community. For instance, the subversive biblical spirituality of Martin Luther King Jr. calls on us to name definite systems that cause a living death for society's marginalized, organize to remove these shackling structures, and proclaim the good news of God's gift of free existence for the world's have-nots. Real people in this world monopolize wealth, resources, and privileges, and their criterion for a healthy community is not the well-being of their fellow citizens but the increase of their wealth and privileges at the expense of the majority. Real black people are suffering from permanent unemployment, underemployment, no heath and medical care, low-quality education, homelessness, domestic violence, rape, daily skin-color discrimination, self-hatred, low self-esteem, loneliness, and lack of human love.

Moreover, African American women's religious experience, at least in fiction, offers an inclusive and holistic spirituality for all of the divinely created body. It recognizes the dwelling of God's grace of life in both church and nonchurch and Christian and non-Christian practices of freedom. In addition, slave spirituality of the folk demands that we serve God through transformation motion. Thus, the spirituality of black theology participates in the growth of God's new creation in our very midst today. Wherever we discover this life-affirming spirituality of poor humanity, we encounter the seeds and signs of God's unfolding liberation of human life. The cry for life from the bottom of society offers all of us hope for the future of the human community. Through heeding this cry, we work with the spirit as it moves in the voiceless and, through them, permeates all levels of the country. Our spirituality comes to the surface when we place ourselves with the divine spirit's presence—that is, with the black poor and with poor people everywhere.

A New Black Heterosexual Male

Too many people within the African American community, church, and black theology believe that gender concerns only women. When the gender issue becomes the center of discussion, most black men, for example, become like corpses. Their tongues grow silent; their bodies drop to a limp posture; and their presence fades into a ghostlike absence. Gender, from their vantage point, relates only to black women. If this logic is true, they reason, then it would be another example of black male sexism to enter the conversation and dominate what is said and not said. The flip side of this belief is that African American men do not have a gender, which is obviously false. Black men have a male gender, so gender refers to both men and women.

Gender differs from sex. Sex speaks to human biology, the genitalia with which each person is born, while gender is defined and determined not by nature but by human culture. Usually sex cannot be changed by human nurturing. Gender construction remains a socialization process influenced by child-rearing and parenting models, peer pressure and positive examples, movies and other media, educational institutions and training organizations, and biblical interpretation and faith communities. Human beings make other human beings into specific male and female genders.

Restated, gender represents both a cultural category and a dynamic process of socialization. Culture includes every aspect of a person's way of believing, thinking, judging, saying, and doing in the world. Culture, moreover, indicates a communal existence. There are no cultures of individuals, only cultures of people, groups, and communities. As a result, we identify an individual based on his or her relation to and interaction with a group. A collective culture contains certain rituals and myths that glue the culture together and help to distinguish one type of culture from another. Furthermore, culture always carries a specific language spoken by a community.

As it is a product of socialization, gender is not formed overnight, nor is it ever a completely finished product. As a vibrant creation, gender follows the ongoing formation of a culture. Cultures of groups do not remain static. In the process of cultures modifying themselves continually, cultures also modify the definition of gender. Consequently, gender becomes a liquid category. It is solid like ice and liquid like water; and it evaporates like mist. Furthermore, socialization tells us that there exists no absolute identification of gender. From this perspective, there are no right or wrong definitions of gender because gender results from how each society socializes people into gender roles.

For black theology of liberation, the key to whatever gender relationships take place in a community is not the description of the genders but the presence or absence of liberation, the ethics of equality, and mutual sharing. In other words, when babies are born, they can become any gender that society socializes them to be. If the privileges that come along with being male rather than female are created by human beings (who go against the spirit of divine liberation), then human beings (who work with the spirit to practice equality) can bring about social change to remove these privileges from the male gender.

Human societies use the dynamic process of socialization to produce a desired gender. The family remains the basic unit for modeling male and female genders. Other factors of influence are schools, sports, visual and audio entertainment, sex roles, jobs and professions, church and other faith institutions, news media, languages, myths, rituals, laws, and race. Especially within the United States of America, the capitalist system sets the broader context for all definitions and formations of gender. This political economic structure maintains a bottom-line culture of profit making at the expense of the majority of the people. The root of the profit culture is private ownership of capital and wealth by a small elite group of families headed by men.

Even more specifically, capitalist democracy means placing a minority of males of a certain race in power positions and as owners of wealth and capital. Immediately we notice a hierarchy of gender as well as class and race. This capitalist democracy hierarchy of the minority over the majority thrives on seeing another human being as someone to be used and dominated for profit and the accumulation of more wealth. From the arrival of the first permanent, English-speaking European colonies in Jamestown, Virginia in 1607 to the constitutional convention in Philadelphia, Pennsylvania in 1787, every foundation of the United States has been based on male superiority. This male gender hierarchy has become so ingrained in the hearts and minds of both women and men that no one even questions the pervasive reality of power positions and wealth owner-ship belonging to a minority U.S. population—men of a certain racial grouping. From 1607 to the twenty-first century, voting and laws have not dislodged this entrenched capitalist, democratic minority of wealthy white men.

In the process of socialization, black men experience a double male gender reality, and both are negative. On one hand, the larger culture of white society defines and portrays black men as subordinate to white men. African American men are socialized as a male gender but as men who are subordinate to the racial supremacy of another male gender. On the other hand, within the African American community, black men are socialized to adopt the normative definition of the male gender that is established and defined by the larger white male culture. As a result, black men strive toward and enjoy male privileges over black women and children within the African American family and community. When black men adopt and implement the patriarchy of the larger white male culture, they can act out a very sinful and potentially deadly force on those around them. Specifically, too often, African American men store up both their frustrations and anger against white men with power and then release these two demons onto the women, children, and other black men within their own families and communities.

To sum up, the white male culture establishes the norm for what it means to be a black man, and African American men pursue this norm. But to imitate this goal outside of the black community and family means accepting one's black manhood as subordinate to white manhood. At the same time, problems with white men with power and wealth lead black men to see their home or their community as their royal domains where they are king and everyone else serves as their subjects. Black men experience a state of victimization by white male superiority, and they simultaneously enjoy male privilege at home and in their neighborhoods.

A system of white male culture in the United States not only sets the norm for what is a male gender, it creates and perpetuates stereotypes about the black male gender. Thus, African American men can never fully reach the norm set by white patriarchy because black men, although males, are not white. At the very same time as they experience this barrier blocking them from realizing the norm, they suffer from a barrage of sinful stereotypes. The visual and audio media in North America image blacks as entertainers through the professions of sports (i.e., Michael Jordan), comedy (i.e., Eddie Murphy), and the military (i.e., Colin Powell). Black men, in the broader culture, are portrayed as being more physical, powerful, and stronger, meaning more sensuous and sexy. As the perfect sexual supermen, African American males are seen as connoisseurs of the sexual act, having the most endurance and physical equipment and possessing an identity motivated by a life in pursuit of the sexual act. Black men, in the logic of these myths, are more emotional, volatile, and unpredictable. Likewise, they lack intelligence and the values of reason, thoughtfulness, academic insight, and deliberate judgment. This false picture goes on to say that African American males are untrustworthy in the areas of wealth and finance, while they have a natural gift for being criminals and engaging in illegal activity. They do not like to work or to work hard and are irresponsible. They are not leaders but followers. In these stereotypes, black males also abandon their children and depend on black women or on white people to support them.

African American men can do one of two things. They can accept this understanding of the black male gender or they can choose to create something new. If they accept the white male culture and practices of male gender and the stereotypes that go along with them, then they should honestly admit that they suffer as victims of a larger structure, but, at the same time, they should admit that they also are making conscious choices to carry out the negative aspects of this structure. This choice has devastating consequences on black women and children in particular. Basically, males who make this choice opt for very harmful power and control strategy and tactics against African American women. These tactics include: persuading black women that they should support the black man at all costs because he is a victim of white male oppression; intimidation, emotional abuse, and isolation of black women; denying and/or minimizing any wrongdoing but blaming the women; using children against women; using male privilege (acting like the king of the castle or making all decisions); and carrying out economic abuse, verbal threats, physical violence, or sexual violence (i.e., through direct physical force or nagging pursuit).

Refusing to opt for this negative and abusive choice, African American men can start to reconstruct what it means to be a new heterosexual male. They can begin first by accepting the love of God that is in all black men. The root of all harmful attitudes and actions against black women and children flow from black men's lack of self-love. But self-love can come to reality only when men understand and feel a love that is greater than any one person. It is a transcendent love, a divine love, a love that comes from the collective body. In this sense, it is not an individual love, but a communal love that floods the very being of the individual as a gift of love proceeding from the community into the soul of the individual. Divine love found within black men corresponds to a sacred love for and from the family and community. Ultimate love or God's love means that God loves black men in spite of the broken vessels that they are.

Such a love has profound implications for the ongoing struggle of African American people to achieve an inclusive and holistic liberation and to practice freedom. The movement for liberation cannot be sustained through the inevitable ups and downs and forward and backward steps and the high successes as well as the stinging defeats unless black men love themselves. And the starting point is recognition and acceptance of God's unconditional love. Indeed, God's love grants the black man a sacred power that gives him allegiance not to any earthly demonic structures or individual authority figures but to something that transcends the boundaries of this world. Equipped with this love and power in one's feelings and one's intellect, in one's heart and one's head, African American men no longer will have to choose negative and abusive options.

On the contrary, the struggle for liberation and the practice of freedom become one's vocation from God. This calling places all social relations, uncontrolled cravings, negative pulls of the black male ego, endless tasks, and incorrect focus on the individual self into perspective. Thus, self-love is not a self-centered practice or feeling where one's worldview and lifestyle become "I pursue money, profit and wealth, therefore I am." Nor does this love indicate a touchy-feely state of being in the world. It is love of self founded on divine love, which subordinates the lifestyle of the individual African American male to enable liberation from negative personal and social structures and a practice of freedom defined by equality. Such a love helps to facilitate a healthy life in the family, in the community, and among all humankind.

A spirituality of love from God acts as the foundation for the definition of the self. Spirituality, however, manifests in the material, real, tangible world. A true heterosexual black male, full of God's love, takes a stand against a host of devious desires and damaging deeds. He speaks out against various discriminations as it pertains to race, gender, class, sexual orientation, and ecological issues. The starting point and yardstick remain justice and freedom for all, beginning with the most oppressed communities in society and the poor. When he lives in the world with this type of talk and walk, he inevitably meets those who wish to maintain their privileges of race, class, gender, sexual orientation, and human cravings over all of God's creation. Therefore, when an African American man stands with the majority—the suffering and vulnerable—

in contrast to the minority—capitalist democracy for the few who own
wealth and power—his very reason for living will be challenged. Those
with power will use different ways to challenge the very idea of God's
love for black men and, consequently, black men's divine-given self-love.
But the more African American men withstand this trial and the more
they feel good about themselves, the more likely there will be healthy
black families and communities. Again, good feelings and healthy
conditions result from engagement in struggle for intentional self-
development and collective transformation. Transformation requires
work; work requires discipline; discipline requires sacrifice; sacrifice
requires motivation from a higher calling; a calling requires a recognition
of being loved; being loved empowers one to love oneself and thereby
free others from the external structures and internal demons in their lives.

For Christians, Jesus stands for this liberation love. God's work in
and through Jesus did not depend on and had nothing to do with the
fact that Jesus was a man biologically. However, the way Jesus developed
his male gender gives us a model for the construction of today's new
black heterosexual male. Because Jesus was so caught up in the mission
of the sacred spirit who had anointed him to be with the poor on the
divine–human journey to practice freedom, Jesus loved himself enough
based on this spiritual vocation. This spirituality of love led to a self-love
that energized Jesus' compassion for the outcasts around him. The most
striking example is revealed in how Jesus talked to, spent time with,
listened to, answered the questions of, healed, and empowered women
to become their full selves. He accepted both male and female disciples.
He commissioned women as well as men to carry out the work of justice
from God. Women became the first preachers to proclaim the liberation
revelation of Jesus as the risen Christ. Jesus ordained them to carry forth
the good news that death caused by a political crucifixion no longer had
the final word. In fact, he broke the status quo boundaries around and

oppressive definitions of what it meant to be both male and female. Any black male who believes and acts as if any black female is secondary does the work of the Antichrist. He goes against the entire birth, life, ministry, and legacy of Jesus the Anointed One. For the followers of Christianity, he has strayed, intentionally or unintentionally, from the path of life.

A theological reconstruction of the black male consists not only of the love of God and the life of Jesus, but also of a realization that God is black for African American males. To be made in the image of God compels black males to make a leap into the blackness of God's essence for them. To worship and surrender total allegiance to something or someone alien to African American males is slow self-destruction and internal spiritual death. A black God affirms every physical characteristic of what the United States calls black. And God says it is good. This realization brings about a subversive move precisely because a spiritual vision, value, and vocation overcomes all the negative stereotypes forced on and propagated against black males. God, as a spirit of equality, manifests in the biological and physical characteristics of African American males. Such a claim can cause a disruption in the minds of men.

Specifically, for too long many black males have been on their knees praying to an old white man with gray hair. On the theological level, this is nonsense since black folk represent the image of God. Therefore, theologically, God by necessity is black if black folk are images of God. And on the psychological and emotional level, praying to a white male god has meant, in the context of North America, too many black people willingly giving their complete selves to the very same image of the system and structure of the supremacy of whites over blacks. This old, gray-haired, white god has been one of the deepest causes for black self-hatred. In this sinful faith of self-hatred, black men can be themselves only by first becoming white. However, neither whites nor blacks are divine in and of themselves. God is black for African American males due to the divine compassion for those on the bottom of society's scale. Again, God's spirit is a spirit of liberation, and it chooses to manifest itself as black to be with the "little ones" of this earth. When African American men go against their black culture, context, and characteristics, they oppose the God of their own human liberation.

Not only is God black, God is both father God and mother God. First of all, the being of God is a spirit. Human speech simply gives various verbal symbols for this divine spirit of liberation and freedom. For example, Jesus, the spirit's decisive revelation for Christians, has various human symbols for divine power—the Savior, the Liberator, Son of God, Son of Man, Mary's Baby, Lily of the Valley, the Shepherd, the Alpha and the Omega, and so forth. Again, human beings receive the spirit and attempt to name the revelation in the best manner possible to paint the presence and power of God. The spirit cannot be contained within one human symbol. The human symbol or description called "father God" represents only one alternative. The male symbol for God—that is, father God—represents only one gender. Left by itself, that excludes 70 percent of the African American church and over 50 percent of the black community. We cannot limit the power and presence of God to one gender. God gave birth to all of humanity and all of creation. God watched over this creation and nurtured it, protected it, taught it, and gave and gives life to it. And so, God's spirit also assumes the human symbol of "mother God."

Theologically, we all are made in God's image. Therefore, black women reflect the female gender of God—mother God. When black men continue to pray to father God only, they are perpetuating and protecting African American men's privileges and expectations of automatic entitlement. Similarly, they continue to subordinate black women and discount the divine reality in their ebony sisters. Men—unfortunately with the help of some women—have established gender hierarchy with a patriarchal god who says he has all power. But this power is limited to one gender. Likewise, this power is limited to hierarchy and not equality. A limited divinity is not God, but the creation of black men who benefit from assuming that African American women are secondary creations of God. A further example of this claim is seen with the clear contrast in the emphasis on God's blackness or Africanness on the part of some black men. Why do these black men not fight as hard for the female gender of God as they struggle for God's black and African dimensions?

An African dimension does occupy a prominent position in the reconstruction of the new black male. African Americans have a mixed background and identity. Centuries have made them integral to what has become the space and time called the United States of America. Simultaneously, however, a black man recognizes and develops the legacy of his African ancestry. The African part of the black male is the very difference that distinguishes his divine identity. In the belief structures of West African peoples—from whom the majority of present-day black Americans are descended—sacred and secular operate together. Otherwise, God would be impotent and missing from some aspect of God's reality. If black men are to live a full life, then they respond to a sacred calling that covers all aspects of everyday living in the United States. Faith stretches beyond a ritual on Sunday or a private prayer. The presence of faith helps the underdogs of society to risk standing up against their earthly oppressors and live as healed and whole beings in the private, public, personal, and political spheres. The God of liberation instructs the new black male to be a man wherever he exists.

Furthermore, the West African legacy gives a black man a sense of respect based on how well he participates with, takes care of, and shares in the African American family. This legacy cuts against the notion of the absent, authoritative, nonvulnerable, domineering North American male who expects entitlement simply because of his biological makeup and a negative affirmative action based simply on his male gender. The West African influence, moreover, centers a black man on the community's well-being. "I am because we are" and "Without community, one is a sub-human animal" become the hallmark of the African American male's lifestyle. The new black male opposes capitalist individualism of me-first and profit-first at the expense of the collective. Such a deadly practice and demonic religion positions one race or gender or class or sexual orientation "first" above others.

PLANTING SEEDS

I am part of two partnerships attempting to talk through and walk into what it means to be a new heterosexual black male. The first group consists of black Christian, heterosexual males, most of whom are married to or in relationships with African American women; and we are all members of black churches.[1] This first instance is what we call a men's house group. Meeting twice a month, on Saturdays at 7:00 A.M., the house group has fourteen members. For us, this space and time provide the conditions for a sacred, holistic perspective on life. We engage in prayer and Bible study, and read liberation materials and theories from a host of disciplines and subject matters. We have read black theology and womanist theology writings; we have spent time covering literature on the plight of and prospects for the black male in America. We have learned about meditation and spiritual formation. We also look at documentary videos from the Reverend Adam Clayton Powell Jr., Martin Luther King Jr., Toni Morrison, Paul Robeson, John Coltrane, Fred Hampton, various black preachers and black churches, and more.

Our sharing on political, cultural, economic, local, national, and international events enables us to reflect individually on the joys (praise reports) and pains (prayer concerns) of each man in the room. In these sacred moments, tears have been shed and discussions have taken place about working with poor black folk and protesting some injustices in the African American community. An ongoing focus is how to become strong black Christian males who can accept the love of God and love of the self and work with the black woman to enhance the African American family and community. However, the ultimate goal is to participate in the well-being of the least in every society of the world. Some of the men involve themselves in areas of direct political work, economic development, or grooming a new generation of young black men through rites-of-passage programs. We have engaged in heated debates on African American parenting and on the ups and downs of Wall Street. Self-criticism has become a part of the program, especially when we discuss how we participate in the liberation of poor blacks; this manifests in the areas of providing jobs, enhancing black health, writing on behalf of the voiceless, proclaiming the gospel of good news and justice for the oppressed, and creating right relationships in other ongoing projects.

The second process of reconstructing black maleness takes place in a black theology and womanist theology course that I teach with my wife, a womanist anthropologist and theologian, Linda E. Thomas. Since 1997 we have been coteaching this course every spring, both at her graduate school and at mine. To our knowledge, this remains the first and only such course cotaught by a black theologian and a womanist theologian. For the curriculum, we have tried to model what black female-black male and black theology and womanist theology relationships mean as practical intellectual disciplines of equality and freedom. Usually, during a ten-week quarter, we spend two weeks on each of five social science categories—race, gender, class, sexual orientation, and ecology.

For instance, when we begin with race, the first week offers the black theologian's perspective on the thought and life of race. Students read theological interpretations of race. During class I, as the black theologian, present a lecture that includes both a social science and a theological perspective on race. Both theoretical and personal experiences are brought to bear in this teaching method. Then my wife, the womanist theologian, responds from a womanist perspective. Next we both engage in a dialogue and, sometimes, a debate. Students enter the conversation after this moment. The next week we continue on race, but the womanist lecture is presented. After the lecture, the black theologian responds; conversation and debate unfold between the two professors, and then students join in. Through this mixture of theory, personal experience, and seeking individual and collective transformation, we strive to clarify, in a scholarly manner, and articulate, through creative visioning, what it means to be new black men and women.

In addition to theoretical constructs and personal stories, I am learning that it is one thing to write and teach about the creation of a new African American male gender. It is another to coteach a course with a womanist, particularly when the womanist is my wife! More specifically, I mean that the course does not end in the classroom; we continue the discussion in our daily living, either verbally or in practice. Since we are both tenured professors, authors, teachers, lecturers, international travelers, and coparents, there really is no credible, compelling, or consistent theological excuse for assuming that the "man" has to do such and such because he is a "man." Therefore, after we discuss the five categories from our classroom teachings, we resume this dialogue on the other side of the threshold of the academic space. In fact, in a very real sense, the title of this course could be "Black Theology and Womanist Theology: From the Kitchen to the Classroom." Indeed, the black male has to learn a gender that opens itself to challenges and transformation in all areas of what it means to be loved by a God who wants liberation for the poor. Some of these inclusive and holistic areas are vulnerability;

protection; intimacy; political protest; self-critique; new forms of leadership both in the home, church, and broader civic society; and other frontiers.

From the perspective of black theology, the question of the creation of a new heterosexual black male gender, flows like a weaving process. It never progresses in a straight line. Like all scientific discoveries, quality relationships, and the implementation of the finest visions, becoming something new is a many-layered process. Sometimes the newness reveals itself as bright as the morning sun or as clear as the brilliance of a black summer night. Other times the struggle falters and goes backward, gripped in the old hand of male privilege. But the foundation of this crucial effort is an openness to what black theology claims so adamantly: that God loves the poor and those who work on justice for the least in society. That is the purpose for the revelation of Jesus the Anointed One on earth. Male chauvinism (the attitude of superiority), male privileges (the practice of this attitude), and patriarchy (the system that exists in spite of how nice individual men are) go against every thing that God, Jesus, and West African ancestors have called black men to be, say, and do. The good news is that African American men will be fully human when black women achieve their full humanity. I am because we are. And we are part of a faith and a tradition that says "God may not come when you call God, but God is always right on time."

PART THREE

BLACK THEOLOGY AND THE WORLD

A Black American Perspective on Interfaith Dialogue in the Ecumenical Association of Third World Theologians

One of the pressing challenges of black theology in the new millennium is to increase interfaith dialogue on a global scale, beginning with various expressions of liberation theologies throughout the world. The only international network of liberation theologians is the Ecumenical Association of Third World Theologians (EATWOT).

The origin of the concept for an international dialogue among liberation theologians in Africa, Asia, and Latin America came from Abbé Oscar. K. Bimwenyi, a Roman Catholic, African student from Zaire studying theology in Louvain, Belgium (1974). As a result of his vision and the preparatory committees composed of representatives from Africa, Asia, and Latin America, the organizing conference that gave rise to the Ecumenical Dialogue of Third World Theologians (later "Dialogue" changed to "Association") took place in Dar es Salaam, Tanzania (August 1976). Since that time, EATWOT has held different continental and intercontinental dialogues with the specific focus on Africa, Asia, Latin America, and the Pacific Islands, and it has taken up the theological significance of race, indigenous peoples, and Third World women.

THE NEED FOR INTERFAITH DIALOGUE

Interfaith dialogue is an urgent call for the present and future for all who are concerned about a healthy survival of the world community for at least three important reasons. First, the overwhelming majority of the earth's people are of different faiths. Likewise, the overwhelming majority of the earth's people live in poverty and are oppressed. If Christianity is based on a faith that takes seriously the full humanity of the poor, then we are faced with the challenge of recognizing one undeniable fact: the majority of the world is non-Christian and poor. Gustavo Gutierrez writes: "The interlocutors of liberation theology are the nonpersons, the humans who are not considered human by the dominant social order—the poor, the exploited classes, the marginalized races, all the despised cultures."[1]

Percentagewise, Asia is the most populous region of the globe. Aloysius Pieris, a theologian from Sri Lanka, has stated at various times that the characteristic features of Asia are its vast poverty and its multifaceted religions. The impact of colonialism and imperialism from the West added greatly to the underdevelopment of Asia. Although the West "exported" its culture, its Christianity has not been able to penetrate or replace the indigenous religions of Asia. Christianity is a minority religion. The great religions and cultures of Asia have stood the test of time, existing before the creation of Christianity and possibly outlasting it. A person cannot be in Asia and not see and feel the presence of a diverse worldview toward nature, music, poetry, human interactions, rituals, history, and so forth. Buddhism, Taoism, Hinduism, Shintoism, Shamanism, Confucianism, Islam, and other faith traditions flow through the veins and hustle and bustle for most of Asia.

In Africa, Islam and African indigenous religions and cultures are all concrete and strong realities. Although Christianity has made stronger inroads here than in Asia, the Christianity of the West has not replaced or erased other faith traditions. In fact, many of the rural peoples of Africa and those in communities immediately outside of the urban areas, still practice indigenous religions and cultures. Even where Christianity has "converted" people, many of these people have combined Christianity with their indigenous religions; in times of crisis, they may rely solely on the indigenous belief systems and cultural practices.

In Latin America, Christianity has become the dominant religion, with Roman Catholicism making the first beachhead and Protestantism being a relatively latecomer. At the same time, in some areas indigenous cultures and people still have their own faiths. In other areas, descendants of Africa have developed unique faiths. And even some of the folk religions have combined indigenous religions with Christianity, particularly with Roman Catholicism.

In the United States, Christianity is without question the dominant form of religious activity. Even though traditional mainstream, white denominations are suffering from a slow membership growth, Christianity is remarkably vibrant. This is so especially in churches for minorities—people of color, or Third World communities within the First World superpower. We see this reality in the growth of Third World Christian communities and in the growth of "Word Churches" or transdenominational churches. Although Christianity has a monopoly, the fastest-growing religion in America is Islam. And some of the great Asian religions and expressions of African indigenous religions are slowly appearing.

The second reason for the importance of interfaith dialogue in EATWOT is the need to take the work and words of Jesus seriously. One of the most quoted biblical passages in EATWOT literature is Luke 4:18ff:

> The Spirit of the Lord is upon me,
> because he has anointed me
> to bring good news to the poor.
> He has sent me to proclaim release for prisoners
> and recovery of sight for the blind,
> to let the oppressed go free,
> to proclaim the year of the Lord's favor.

This statement by Jesus is seen as the core of the gospel message. To believe in Jesus is to walk the way of Jesus. In the world today, which people are lame, or blind, in jail, suffering from physical abuse, unemployed and underemployed, lonely and unloved? These are victims from all faiths. If we are to follow the way of Jesus and be with the poor, because that is where Jesus resides, then we are not bound by church doctrines or institutional restriction. Consequently, to be with Jesus will mean, in many cases, not ever being in a Christian institution or context.

Furthermore, this divine revelation, which dwells among the poor in their struggle for full humanity, is not contained only in the way of Jesus. If God is the spirit of freedom for the vulnerable in society, then this spirit has to be active as an event and process of struggle even where the name of Jesus is not known. We cannot confine our experience of God within human-made doctrines or beliefs. Again, Gutierrez instructs us: "Liberation theology categorizes people not as believers or unbelievers but as oppressors or oppressed."[2] In fact, to use church tradition or a narrow biblical interpretation to say that God is only or exclusively where Jesus is present is to reduce God's power for, love of, and presence with those who hurt the most in the world. God continues to be with marginalized communities seeking a life of abundance against the reign of evil and mammon wherever it shows its ugly face. Among the cries of all the discarded peoples, God reveals God's self in all faiths around the globe. To deny this is to possibly participate in a new form of imperialism—a Christocentric imperialism against the majority of the other faiths on earth. As Aloysius Pieris correctly claims:

> The vast majority of God's poor perceive their ultimate concern and symbolize their struggle for liberation in the idiom of non-Christian religions and cultures. Therefore, a theology that does not speak to or speak through this non-Christian peoplehood is an esoteric luxury of a Christian minority. Hence, we need a theology of religions that will expand the existing boundaries of orthodoxy as we enter into the liberative streams of other religions and cultures.[3]

Finally, interfaith dialogue is crucial because the international economy of monopoly capitalism, the destruction of indigenous cultures, racial discrimination against darker-skinned peoples around the world, the oppression of women, and the attack on the earth's ecology are global dynamics that do not limit themselves to the Christian community. When American monopoly capitalist corporations seek cheap labor in Asia, particularly among Asian women, these companies are not concerned about whether the workers are Buddhist or Christian. The bottom line is using their labor power in order to make profit. When American monopoly capitalist corporations pursue investments in Nigerian oil, they are not concerned if the workers there are Muslim, indigenous religious practitioners, or Christians. Finance capital can own both a textile factory in Indonesia staffed by Buddhist women while simultaneously owning an oil refinery in Africa staffed by Islamic workers. In other words, global capital has already begun the process of interfaith interactions among many of the poor of this earth. But it is a dialogical process where healthy faith conversations are too often subservient to the needs of profit and the accumulation of more profit and capital.

HOW TO CARRY OUT INTERFAITH DIALOGUE

In an interfaith dialogue, it is important to take indigenous cultures seriously. Many peoples of the Third World do not have a word for "religion" because faith is not a separate sphere. (This contrasts with the European Enlightenment's definition of religion, where sacred practices differ from secular activities.) Faith is part of the culture; it is part of everyday behavior. It is lived out daily in relation to the air, fire, rain, flowers, mountains, water, food, animals, the living-dead ancestors, the unborn, and other family relations. So dialogue begins not by recognizing institutional organizations, church traditions, or doctrines but by seeing people and their physical bodies, where they are at and how they live out their faith in their total commonplace affairs. Many poor Christians often say certain doctrines and perform certain rituals that look superficially like Christianity, but in fact, they are mixing pre-Christian religious and cultural belief systems and practices with Christianity. To think that such Christians are Christians only because of the Sunday church services and the various celebrations of the Christian calendar events is to miss the rest of their usual activities from Monday through Saturday. Theologian Esau Tuza (from the Solomon Islands) comments on the persistence and mixing of indigenous religions alongside and with Christianity:

Our worship based on ancestral belief is not dead. Our ancestors are very much alive and thriving. They make their way to the church buildings via the grave and the cross. We pay them traditional respect through reverence and prayer. They follow us from the church buildings to the world where we live and witness with the rest of God's people, knit together in love and service. Only Christian colonialists, who seek to find God in Western garb, will not be able to see this truth. Despite this, of course, we consciously or unconsciously live side by side with our ancestors.[4]

Both the general facts that most of the world's poor, who are non-Christian, often do not have a word for "religion" and that many Christian poor still have a way of faith outside or alongside of or mixed with Christianity point to the need to see and hear and feel faith as an inclusive behavior everyday for the poor.

Because most of the world's poor talk about their faith (both in societies that do not rely primarily on written texts and those that do), interfaith dialogue has to be sensitive to the language of oppressed people. For example, Asia can be divided into at least seven major linguistic zones, the most of any continent. There is, first of all, the Semitic zone, concentrated in the western margin of Asia. The Ural-Atlantic group is spread all over Asiatic Russia and northwest Asia. The Indo-Iranian stock and Dravidian ethnic groupings have their cultural habitat in southern Asia. The Sino-Tibetan region, by far the largest, extends from Central Asia to the Far East. The Malayo-Polynesian wing opens out to the southeast. Last but not least is the unparalleled Japanese, forming a self-contained linguistic unit in the northeastern tip of Asia.[5]

Language is not merely a medium or method of expressing beliefs, like some type of neutral tool that does not play a decisive role in the process and creation of faith. Language is key to understanding and experiencing the ways people believe and live with their God of hope, survival, and liberation. For people involved in interfaith dialogue, multiple languages, therefore, are important to know. EATWOT and other institutions concerned about the realignment of power relations need to carry out interfaith dialogue not only in the languages that colonizers and missionaries brought to the Third World. They must translate the people's own languages.

In addition, participants in interfaith dialogue need to find a way to hear and speak the indigenous languages of people. Language is part of the culture of a people, and culture is the context of faith. Language gives us a feel for how people live their lives. It helps us understand the different shades of meaning that they experience regularly with God. Language speaks to the role of men and women in a society of believers. For example, in some indigenous cultures and in some African communities, there is no separate pronoun for female and male. This is radically different from the patriarchal language of English, which not only distinguishes between male and female but consistently refers to God as "he," meaning that females are made in the image of a male God. This is not just a question of semantics or sentence construction. It speaks, more importantly, to who has power in society and whether that power is equally distributed among people in a culture. Moreover, to speak the language that expresses the disparate faiths of different peoples is to be involved in the rhythm of that community. Some languages are spoken very fast with diverse accents; others are spoken more slowly. Both are dynamics that express the common conduct of various peoples. And these ways of living are integrally linked to how and what communities believe.

To share with multiple faiths, we will have to see, hear, and listen to varied cultural expressions of these faiths. Legends and folktales serve as a major way of keeping together a group's identity, dreams, tradition, morals, and connections to the divine. Some tales or dreams speak of liberation by using a small animal or animals that outsmart bigger animals. Other tales are about heroic figures who are larger than the ordinary, part human and part supernatural. Legends and folktales give groups inspiration, perspective on the immediate and current problems they face, and hope that there is a force greater than themselves who has preceded them and will be there after they have departed from this world.

In other words, people can get hope, energy, and determination from their own indigenous stories. Poetry—both its content as well as its form—also expresses faith. Similarly, songs are basic to all societies of believers and are extremely significant in the interfaith dialogue. Plays and skits speak about what different communities believe in, too. And finally, peoples in most cultures have developed a certain folk wisdom that is not learned through books but accumulates over long periods of time from the trials and errors of daily life. It is the wisdom learned through frequent practices. These are the unrefined expressions of faith that are so prevalent in the beliefs of the people that, to them, they are simply common sense or usual occurrences. Faith in cultural expressions is, then, crucial for the majority of the world's people.

Interfaith dialogue also will be helped when participants pay attention to how people carry out their ordinary lives of survival. How are different faiths affected by how people produce and reproduce their lives? In rural areas without running water, how does the routine ritual of taking buckets to the river or to a common water faucet impact the faith of those who do this regularly? How does it impact the times of day that they worship? Does this give them a different perspective on nature, human purpose, and the divine? And how might they envision all of these interacting? Why are certain animals considered sacred? Is it because of particular traditions, because of the scarcity of these animals in the society, or because these animals symbolize something else like sacrifices?

For instance, the South African theologian Gabriel M. Setiloane claims the following about the relation between humans and animals as seen in creation stories of African indigenous religions: "Humans emerge out of the hole in the group *together:* men, women, children with their animals. This stresses the uniqueness and right-to-be of every group and species. Even animals have a God-given right-to-be, and must, therefore, not be exterminated."[6]

What do the relationships among crops, agricultural seasons, and rain and thunder suggest about people's faith? Is it possible for a healthy interfaith dialogue to occur if participants are not aware of how God or other expressions of the divine reveal themselves through rain and thunder and the success of planting and harvest? If people's experience of that which is greater than themselves is linked closely with whether their communities eat or drink, then the presence of the divine with the poor has to be seen in how they grow and harvest their crops for survival. Theologian Manuel M. Marzal observes the following about the Indian culture of the Quechua in southern Peru. He finds that, despite modernization, their precolonial culture remains very much intact in the following ways:

> cultivation of the soil and raising cattle as the basic economic activities; vertical control of the ground to safeguard its use by the various ecological levels; reciprocity as a fundamental norm for coexistence in this environment; kinship and the compadre system as the basis of social organisation; dualistic criteria in the conceptualisation of social life; use of the Quechua language as the basic means of communication; communion with nature through the deification of the earth and the hills that mark the boundaries of the dwelling place of each community; celebration of the patron saint's day as the most important religious rite, which carries with it certain implications about the distribution of the communal power and wealth.[7]

The emotional makeup of diverse communities is also important. How do people deal with grief, pain, and death? Is there some way of finding out how the community and its faith respond when babies or children die? Do they ask questions of God, other spirits, or ancestors? Does the faith community become weaker in its relation to the divine? What ways do they hold themselves together and what answers do they provide for or receive from their God? What does their faith tell them about the fate of the child or baby who is dead, and what do they believe about the people whose child is now gone? Understanding how people celebrate also aids the dialogue. What is valuable in a community that causes a people to celebrate and be thankful—is it the birth of a child or of a male child; the success of getting food; a wedding that brings together different families; the rite of passage of girls and boys into womanhood and manhood; or an annual ritual of remembering an elder who has passed away? Likewise, how people laugh, why they laugh, and what causes them to laugh can help in finding out more about the faith of others.

In the same way, dance plays an important role in sharing faith. The body movement and gestures tell the story of the community's life-and-death concerns. For instance, when Ruth M. Stone, a visitor to the Kpelle people of Liberia, was initiated into the experiences of this indigenous culture, she learned how music is an integral part of the culture as a spiritual experience. Reporting on her initiating process, Stone concluded:

> A quality performance, said a number of Kpelle people, depends upon the aid of the supernatural. Really good singers, dancers, or instrumentalists could not operate at such a level unaided. Normal human performance was simply much more ordinary. As I apprenticed myself to learn to play the koning, a triangular frame zither, I learned firsthand

about this. At my third lesson when I was still playing rather crudely, Bena, my tutor and an expert koning player, said, "You need to know about the spirit. As soon as you start playing fine, it will not be you who is playing but the thing is behind you [spirit]". And so I learned concretely of the supernatural part in all excellent music.[8]

Here music defines the identity of the community in relation to its connection to divine spirit. The releasing of the self and the body to the instructions and presence of the spirit was the means of becoming fully oneself.

Social relations of power within societies also determine diverse ways of believing. Who has power and decision-making privileges? Who owns the wealth and the major sectors of the economy? Who has the final say or the main voice about how the goods and services are distributed? Who interprets how the community relates to the resources provided by nature? Who determines what in nature is sacred and who can touch these sacred objects? How does the authority of the sacred person get passed down from generation to generation? Are things shared in common, or are there specific roles for certain people or parts of society? Are these roles fixed, and if so why? Is there any mobility in a community, and who is mobile and who is not? Any interfaith dialogue must make explicit how power is allocated among people in a society.

Furthermore, in the interfaith dialogue, participants need to be aware of the different ways how race and dark and light skin impact a community of believers. If dark skin is equated with evil or not being in the interest of the group, this will affect the beliefs of both the lighter-skin people as well as the darker-skin people. Usually it says something about the color of the divinity or representatives of the divinity that the population worships.

For instance, for over 50,000 years, black people have been in the southwest Pacific (Australia and the surrounding islands of Papua New Guinea, Tasmania, the Solomon Islands, Vanuatu, New Caledonia, and Fiji). Despite the success of European missionaries in introducing Christianity, indigenous and precolonial black culture and black faith still persist. In his call for a better understanding of "black humanity," theologian Aruru Matiabe (from Papua) writes:

> The religious beliefs and ceremonies of blacks in their natural state imbued life with profound meaning and did allow for true communion with the divine. White Christians could have found much there that was valuable had they looked before so many of them denounced it as totally wrong. Every person is a creature of God, and this God does not belong only to whites. Blacks have a spirit just as whites do; skin color does not matter because, not only are we members of the same species biologically speaking, but also we have the same Spirit within us. . . . It was thus wrong-headed for whites to have expected blacks to renounce their past . . . and completely accept the ways and the god of the European.[9]

Color not only speaks directly to which God is present, but it also helps to determine the psychology of different races or shades of color among people. It raises the question of a hierarchy of worth. By determining this hierarchy, those interested in interfaith dialogue can learn who is thought to be the most worthy of receiving the resources and privileges that God has provided for that community.

Related to race is caste, which also determines discrimination. A clear example are the Dalit, the Black Untouchables, of India. India's ruling group, a minority population known as the Hindu Brahmin, has established a hierarchy in social relations where the Dalit suffer not only because of their dark color but also because they are either at the bottom or outside of the caste system. The Hindu Brahmin ideology sees the Dalit as pollution.

> Every Hindu believes that to observe caste and untouchability is his dharma—meaning his religious duty. But Hinduism is more than a religious system. It is also an economic system. In slavery, the master at any rate had the responsibility to feed, clothe and house the slave and keep him in good condition lest the market value of the slave should decrease. But in the system of untouchability, the Hindu take no responsibility for the maintenance of the Untouchable. As an economic system, it permits exploitation without obligation.[10]

The author of this statement, V. T. Rajshekar, continues by claiming that "the Indian Black Untouchable not only cannot enter the house of a Hindu, but even his very sight or shadow is prohibited by the dictates of the Hindu religion."[11]

The issue of gender is closely connected to the different issues surrounding race and, likewise, must be taken seriously in all interfaith dialogues. Often men occupy positions of authority, control, and ownership in the society, in the family, and in their connection to women. In the rituals of faith, men frequently function as the official representatives of the divine. This gives them the privilege to have an authority to represent, speak for, be closer to, be an interpreter of, or even embody the divine purpose within the community of faith. In other faith gatherings that rely on a written sacred text, men are able to interpret the mysteries of these texts if women are not recognized equally as keepers of the text. This can give males access to the major source of power—the power to speak for God, other divine spirits, the ancestors, or nature.

Land, as a key part of nature, will have to be at the center of dialogue with indigenous communities of believers. This is true because theologically their religions hold earth in high regard and because politically they are fighting capitalist governments and corporations that have stolen their land. Religious scholar Rosario Battung confirmed this fact for the indigenous of Asia:

> Land remains central to our indigenous people's quest for wholeness of life. In their continuing struggle for ancestral domain vis-à-vis the government's development schemes, they have maintained a deep reverence for nature. Nature involves not only land and resources but the very life and culture of indigenous people. To take away the land would mean their death, for land is not commodity but home.[12]

Indigenous people place the land at the center of their cultures and faith, whether they consider earth as mother or believe in tales depicting humanity and animals emerging from a hole in the ground. The earth is sacred.

Dialoguing around what is spirituality is also crucial in interfaith conversations. From a liberation perspective, spirituality means not relying on accumulating material things and not seeking profit as the goal in life. Spirituality is the integration of the emotional, physical, and intellectual, and it is the communal sharing of all the resources God has given humanity. Spirituality is both an interior process of becoming closer to liberation and an exterior process of struggling for liberation.

Internally, this means being free from harmful desires and negative thoughts about oneself, others, and nature. The Tseltal, an indigenous Indian people of Mexico, say the following about lack of internal harmony: "of a person who is indecisive, worried or two-faced they say cheb yo'tan—two hearts; of a suspicious or distrustful person ma'spisi-luk yo'tan—one who does not act with his or her whole heart; of a jealous person ti'ti 'o'tantayel—a biting heart."[13] Wholeness on the inside defines liberation as freedom from personal addictions, includ-ing addictions to material accumulation and profit. The interior freedom, in addition, allows us to achieve an internal feeling of peace, power, and love of one's self so that one's mind, soul, and body can focus on serving the poor in the process of liberation.

The exterior spirituality means to make a conscious decision to be with and support the economically poor and oppressed in their move-ment for liberation. Divine spirit is embodied, incarnated, and repre-sented by the plight and success of the least in society as they struggle to survive and reach their full humanity.

In fact, the spirit of liberation is the common basis for an interfaith dialogue whose purpose is liberation. When we meet other faiths, how is the spirituality of liberation manifested in them? How do the poor and the marginalized in a society struggle to reach their full potential; that is to say, what is their movement to become fully what they have been created to be? At the same time as they reach their full humanity, how are they growing in such a way that full humanity helps nature to be healthy? Anne Pattel-Gray, an Australian Aboriginal, gives one answer when she writes: "Our spirituality begins from the day we are born, and continues in how we live, how we care for our brothers and sisters, how we deal with our extended family, and how we care for God's creation. It is all balanced and cannot be divided."[14] A liberation spirituality as the norm in interfaith dialogue means that the oppressed have internal peace, justice, and freedom that is expressed in the external social relations with their families, communities, and nature. This liberation will be obvious in the new status of women and of darker-skin people, the communal ownership of all resources, connections to the elderly and children, and the well-being of nature.

CHAPTER SIX

The Religion
of Globalization

The many different interactions between globalization and religion can be approached from a variety of theological perspectives and ethical practices. The World Council of Churches (WCC) is one such model. The WCC constitutes the largest transnational institutional manifestation of diverse communities of Christian faith. It encompasses the denominations of Protestantism (Episcopal, Presbyterian, Methodist, Congregational, Baptist, etc.), structural dialogue with the Roman Catholic Church, a strong presence of and leadership by Eastern Orthodox churches, and an assortment of new syncretized or indigenous forms of Christian religions from Africa, Asia, and Latin America. The WCC takes seriously the Christian imperative to make all people followers of Jesus Christ, the light of the world. In this regard, Christianity perceives its domain as a form of discipleship on a global stage where, by way of the preached word, theological instruction, sacramental ritualization, iconographic representation, and a persistent witness of love, justice, and reconciliation, the message of Jesus the Christ will truly become the embodied vision of a new and ultimate future for all.

The Council for a Parliament of the World's Religions, in contrast, pursues the multilateral engagement of diverse communities of faith— from African indigenous religions, the great religions of Asia, Islam, Judaism, Protestantism and Catholicism, to any forms of faith expressions on the global scale that agree to civil conversation through mutual encounter. Whereas the WCC might have an evangelistic prescriptive dimension, the Parliament pursues conversations across national borders that are guided by enlightened dialogue in which each religion offers its unique gifts to the universal human community regardless of any particular doctrinal demands and tradition's commands. Moreover, again in contrast to the WCC, the Parliament refrains from any explicit involvement in political problems. Its primary aim is to broaden the number of interlocutors so that changes in the human condition follow logically from more and more people getting to know one another. The metaphor and reality of a parliament mean respectful interchange and exchange of the broadest possible belief systems and faith communities throughout the world. The wider the contact and knowledge of the other, the increased possibilities of living together in harmony.

A third paradigm of religion and globalization contact appears in the Pluralism Project, which is located at Harvard University.[1] Here the revelation of globalization is implosion. Instead of seeking various ways to unify religious communities outside of the United States, the Project examines the increased religious diversity in the United States, focusing especially on the growing multidimensional nature of religions brought by immigrant groups. The analysis does not investigate how the powerful colonial center reaches out to religions in the colonies or geographic peripheries of the world. Quite the opposite; instead of ascertaining the

dominant religions' missionary explosion outward all over the earth—
especially Christian world evangelization from North America to the
Third World—the Pluralism Project observes implosion: how non-
Christian religions from the rest of the world, particularly from the Third
World, are undergoing a process of potential long-term saturation of the
American domestic Christian landscape. The Project seeks to discern
how Americans of all faiths are crafting a positive pluralism.

This chapter pursues an alternative claim. The argument is that
globalization of monopoly finance capitalist culture itself is a religion.
Such a religious system feeds on the most vulnerable people in the world
theater. Consequently, a theology of liberation is one necessary response
to the rapacious appetite of globalization qua religion. The Ecumenical
Association of Third World Theologians (EATWOT) signifies this
response.[2] Most of this chapter defines the contours of globalization as
a religion. At the end, I examine the schematic theological position of
EATWOT.

GLOBALIZATION AS A RELIGIOUS SYSTEM

Religion is a system of beliefs and practices comprised of a god (the
object of one's faith), a faith (a belief in a desired power greater than
oneself), a religious leadership (which determines the path of belief),
and religious institutions (which facilitate the ongoing organization of
the religion). Religion also has a theological anthropology (which
defines what it means to be human), values (which set the standards to
which the religion subscribes), a theology (the theoretical justification
of the faith), and revelation (the diverse ways that the god manifests
itself in and to the world).[3]

God, more specifically, is the ultimate concern of a community of
believers. This god is the final desire and aim that surpasses and

circumscribes all other secondary realities, dreams, wants, and actions. It controls all things and motivates its believers to gear their entire lives in pursuit of and in obedience to it. It subordinates believers and all of creation to the power of itself. It possesses the believers and compels them to pursue it because it has the ability never to be totally fulfilled and never to be finally contained and controlled by its followers. Faith in an ultimate power greater than oneself, moreover, is the ground of being for its believers. The foundation of their essence and identity rests on this god. Their very being in the world is determined by god. In a word, this god is the highest life-and-death concern.

Globalization is the existence of the United States as the sole superpower throughout the earth and in outer space programs. No longer blocked by the challenges of the former U.S.S.R., the United States defines the standards in technology, finance, diplomacy, culture, the military, the ecology, and political government. Even countries that differ from America focus their energies against it. In their opposition, countries still must engage the United States at some global level.

The god of the religion of globalization is the concentration of monopoly finance capitalist wealth. The god of globalization, in this sense, is not merely a belief in the accumulation of capital for private possession by owners operating inside of one country; that stage is a lower one in the development of capitalism. On the contrary, the god of globalization embodies the ultimate concern where there is a fierce belief in the intense concentration, in a few hands, of finance capitalism on the world stage. It is an extreme expression of the private ownership and control of capital in various forms of wealth spurred on by the rapid movement of finance and capital on a global scale. Monopoly wealth is a power in its own right that makes its adherents bow down to it and pursue any means necessary to obtain it. All who believe in it are possessed by it; it is the final goal above all else.

Furthermore, it is transcendent; it has no allegiances to individuals, institutions, or boundaries. "Far more wealth than ever before is stateless, circulating wherever in the world the owner can find the highest return. Thus, spending by investors in industrialized countries on overseas stocks increased 197-fold between 1970 and 1997, and each nation's capital market is beginning to merge into a global capital market."[4] This god of monopoly finance capitalist wealth is not confined or defined by anything except its own internal drive for increased concentration of more wealth. Like a supernatural phenomenon, it does manifest in the tangible (hence its immanence). At the same time, the tangible does not exhaust its power (hence its transcendence). Ultimately, the telos—the final providence of a god—is to reproduce itself by making the entire world of humanity and the ecology subordinate to the intense concentration of monopoly capital. Instead of characterizing itself as love, liberation, justice, or reconciliation, this god is mammon.

The small groups of families who comprise the religious leadership in the religion of globalization are located mainly in the United States. They are a select group set aside, like priests, who maintain knowledge of the laws of this god and what it requires of its followers. Their knowledge signifies a certain type of gnosis—insider information, networking among each other, direct access to the power and benefits of their god, the larger parameters and long-term vision, setting the pace in the pursuit of this god, defining what it means to be a true believer, confidence to determine the lives of their followers, influencing public opinion, and the decision-making power over who and who will not enter the priesthood. For instance, the United Nations Development Program's "Human Development Report of 1992" defined this priesthood by way of income distribution: "The richest 20% of the world's population receives 82.7% of the total world income, while the poorest 20% receives only 1.4%. The gap between the rich and the poor is continuing to grow."[5] The richest 225 individuals in the world constitute a combined wealth over $1 trillion. This amount is equal to the annual income of the poorest 47 percent of the world's population. And the three richest people on earth own assets surpassing the combined gross domestic product of the forty-eight least-developed countries.[6] The priests are the minute group of families who privately own, control, and distribute wealth and the means of production.

There are numerous religiouslike institutions that facilitate the transcendent flow of monopoly finance capital. However, three in particular comprise what can be termed a trinity: the World Trade Organization (WTO), international banks (including the International Monetary Fund [IMF] and the World Bank), and monopoly capitalist corporations. The WTO exists to monitor and enhance international trade. Its name connotes that it is an objective world body adjudicating and massaging global trade for the world's peoples, perhaps by pursuing a scientific neutral line of interaction. Yet it functions in the interest of the god of capitalist wealth. Determined to a great extent by American interests, the WTO is that part of the trinity maintaining an unequal balance of trade mainly by advocating and practicing free trade so that the god in the religion of globalization can have unimpeded free access to the developed world and the Third World (Africa, Asia, the Caribbean, Latin America, and the Pacific Islands). It pushes for an increased consumer market for finance capitalist investment. Moreover, it is influenced by and weighted toward that small group of priests of globalization's religion.

The second person of the trinity—international banks along with the IMF and the World Bank—serves to set conditions of loans, particularly to the Third World, so that underdeveloped countries become converted to the global religion. Third World countries receive financial loan packages that demand that they shift resource focus away from domestic priorities to repay international loans. In order to repay the interest on original debt (not including the principal), developing countries take out more loans from mainly U.S. monopoly financial capitalist corporations, then more loans to meet the interest repayment schedule of the second loan, which was acquired to meet the dept repayment schedule of the first loan. Indeed, the deeper the debt, the more loans are needed to continue the repayment process on earlier loans. Once the initial initiation rite of loan procurement is accomplished, Third World countries become full (dependent) members of this global religion. In this sense, international banks are like missionaries who travel the world seeking new converts. And similar to the history of Christianity, the indigenous ways of being in the world are replaced, wiped out, or syncretized with the arrival of this foreign religion. Monopoly capitalist corporations (MNCs), the third person of the trinity, are the direct institutional instruments of the priests of this religion. The MNC signifies an interlocking ownership and control of wealth and finances. It can interlock wealth across and within industries; and it can have headquarters in one country with subsidiary "missionary" outposts in other nations. For instance, U.S. soft drink companies also have part ownerships in concentrated fruit products, newspapers, the media, airlines, television stations, Hollywood studios, clothing manufacturing, fast food lines, and automobile companies. Such a concentration of wealth enables the MNC to shift wealth and investments throughout the globe to undercut, underprice, and buy off an entire range of companies in the Third World, thereby "proselytizing" more members and areas of the earth into the religion.

Like all religions, the religion of globalization advances a theological anthropology. (Theological anthropology defines and regulates what it means to be a human being in a religious system.) What does a god require of human beings in order for them to be human? The god of globalization calls on the priests of this religion to act out an ontology (e.g., the very being of who they are) in the quest for the epitome of the ideal person. Such a human being is one who has the most concentrated financial wealth accumulation on a global scale. Ideally, since religions have a proclivity for utopia, a small group would control the world's capital. Here capital includes both the majority of the human population—real people—and the ecology—the earth's natural and human-made resources. In the future utopia on earth, all social relations among human beings will be defined by the god of concentrated wealth. In other words, to be a human being is to fit on an unequal scale of wealth ownership. Wealth redistribution goes upward into the possession of a small group of citizens.

In contrast, theological anthropology for the majority of the world suggests another reality of what it means to be human in the religion of globalization. Prior to globalization, especially in Third World indigenous communities, human beings were valued for who they were as members of the human race created by some divine power. Now globalization rebaptizes them into a new man and woman, where the measure of worth becomes what one consumes. Globalization's religion forges new tastes and sensibilities throughout the world while it attempts to manufacture one transcendent culture—the culture of market consumption. A true human being becomes one who actually possesses commodities or one whose goal in life is to do so. Despite the fact that the vast majority of Third World peoples live in poverty, the religion of globalization attempts to transform them into adherents of the faith by inducing in them a desire to perceive themselves as owning the products from the developed capitalist world. This fact touches the core issue of the new religion, which wants people not only to purchase products but to reconceive of themselves as people. To change into something new, various groups must, besides redirecting their purchasing habits, refeel who they are in the present and reenvision their possibilities for the future. Communities are baptized into a lifestyle to fulfill the desire for commodities and to follow further the commodification of desires.

Globalization pursues relentlessly this refashioning of the new man and woman throughout the globe. It seeks a homogenized monoculture of the market to bring about the transformation of people who are valued in themselves to people who are determined by their dependency on commodities. A world culture producing one definition of what it means to be a human being is predicated on serving the market. The market of monopoly capitalism benefits the small group of priests in the religion of globalization. In contrast, most of the world's population are left out. "The pragmatic [and positive] analysis of economists and financiers are based on the principle of exclusion. Growing poverty and exclusion have [be]come a dominant social and political development of our era. Inequality and exclusion are not distortions of the system. They are a systematic requisite for growth and permanence."[7] Restated, within the religion of globalization, most peoples of the world are excluded from utilizing the earth's resources, are victimized by extreme social polarization, and are blocked from reaching their full human potential.

The spreading of different values is closely linked to theological anthropology. As one redefines oneself, by accepting the new religion's reconfiguring of the human person, one internalizes values appropriate to the new man or woman. The point of the religion of globalization is to craft new values to accompany the new person. First is the value of individualism. If monopoly finance capital is to succeed as the new god throughout the earth, it has to decouple the idea, particularly in Third World indigenous cultures, that the individual is linked to, defined by, accountable to, and responsible for his or her family and extended family. A sense of communalism and sacrifice of individual gain for the sake of a larger community stands in stark contradiction to the new religion of globalization. Once an individual converts to the new religion and reorients his or her self-worth and feeling of worthiness to a mode of individual gain, regardless of the well-being of those around him or her, this person has successfully undergone the rite of confirmation into the new religion and has accepted faith in the new god as a personal lord and savior. The value of individualism (e.g., individual gain by any means necessary) is central to the god of monopoly finance capitalism.

Individualism opens up the additional value of accumulation of things for the individual's primary benefit. In other words, gaining and amassing personal possession as a means of acquiring more personal possessions flows from a focus on the self for the self. This acquisitive desire manifests itself in diverse ways. It downplays sharing. It weakens the art of negotiation and compromise. It blinds a vision of mutuality. And it fosters a utilitarian way of being in the world where people, places, and things become tools for and stepping-stones toward increased personal profit. On the political level, such a value breeds a type of "monopoly capitalist democracy" constituted by subordination of the many for the few. This form of democracy employs the many to attain more resources for the few. As a political value, such a democracy equates the common good and the larger civic welfare with pragmatic results for the elite. In the economic sphere, it is an internal feeling that prompts the individual to pursue profit to gain more personal profit. It privileges the importance of commodities and material goods. Economic wealth is valued as one of the highest virtues in the definition of the new human being. Akin to an addiction (when left to mature), it motivates, gnaws at, and compels the new converted person to make life-and-death decisions based on the amount of wealth he or she has. The ownership of wealth commodities and/or the hunger for this ownership controls the person's perception of the worth of life and death.

A positive worldview of individualism and the thirst for commodities lead more easily to valuing the United States and other developed capitalist countries. These centers epitomize a culture and perfection of individualism and commodification. When a person accepts and seeks to imitate the attributes of globalization, he or she tends to gravitate toward the geographical and imaginative locations where those values have advanced more fully. The "West" becomes a place, like a utopia, of meaning to fulfill one's theological anthropology. Those in Third World countries who are able to migrate toward western cities bring their worth as human beings closer to a realized individualism and commodification. The elite remaining in developing countries deploy energies and resources, metaphorically or literally, to purchase or imitate the latest thought forms, things, and lifestyles from New York, Paris, or London. For the overwhelming majority of people in the Third World, the values of globalization breed the conditions for the possibility of desiring those things from the West. The religion of the new human being moves one's senses through space, time, and imagination to the "altars" of the monopoly finance capitalist god of concentrated wealth. Lacking god's material gifts, one values and feeds on the desire for materiality.

And this god has a theology. Theology denotes a rational understanding, justification, and meaning making of a god. In religious discourse, theology takes on an added sense of justification of one's faith to the public. What rationale does one give to account for one's faith in the public domain of competing and conflictual faith claims? What system of views, theoretical argumentation, and coherent conclusions does one advance in common conversation? Theology makes sense of faith in god. If the god is concentrated monopoly wealth, then how does one imagine and explain faith in this god? The theology of neoliberalism is the primary elaboration and justification of concentrated financial wealth.

Neoliberalism as the theological justification for the god of the religion of globalization has three prominent doctrines. First is the emphasis on free markets—a movement to open up global markets, especially in the Third World.[8] Actually the market is not free for all countries because as transnational corporations enter or deepen their hold in the domestic economies of developing countries, corporations are free to repatriate their profit from loans and investment at the expense of the poor and the market share of local businesses. The criterion upon entry into a market is to adhere to and pursue concentrated monopoly wealth. However, some form of freedom does occur for developing countries. They enjoy the freedom to restructure domestic growth based on linkages to export industries. Yet these exports are intertwined with serving the needs of the developed capitalist countries, a process that disrupts the economic planning for domestic prosperity. Export orientation, furthermore, is driven by the quest for diverse forms of foreign currency. Thus free markets grant favorable terms for transnational monopoly corporations to enter developing countries and create unfavorable terms for developing countries' efforts at exporting. Free markets translate into unrestricted entry of the god of globalization.

Privatization, the second theological justification, is a condition imposed on Third World countries by transnational corporations. If a developing country opens its market borders, it has to agree to refocus domestic resources of the state government away from providing health, education, welfare, jobs, and other safety nets for its citizens. Instead, the state's accumulated resources go into repaying debt on loans invested by monopoly capitalists, who create whatever conditions corporations require to enhance other types of investment in the developing country. Consequently, neoliberalism theology promotes, as one condition for various investments, the practice of privatization of social services for the vast majority of the people; for the Third World, this means the poor. Not only do domestic private businesses seek to substitute for the previous role of the government, but transnational corporations also profit by providing private services to the public, at least to those who can afford the costs. However, exceptions to the transformed function of Third World states do occur. Local governments, as additional conditions for foreign investments, undergird the environment of monopoly financial corporate presence by way of tax breaks, transfer payments, an increased military, and a burgeoning prison network—the latter being geared to the unemployed, opposition forces, and criminal sectors.

The third theological justification is deregulation. The religion of globalization offers a "commonsense" explanation for this final justification. It seems to "make sense" that a government enmeshed in regulations implies a heavy state bureaucracy that consumes scarce resources, time, and personnel that could be deployed more efficiently elsewhere in the domestic economy. Thus, if Third World countries are to enjoy the benefits (e.g., "grace") of the god of monopolized capitalist wealth, the theology of neoliberalism calls for stripping governments of their historic role of regulating the harmful effects of business practices imposed on people and the ecology. Transnational corporations demand, in return for investment, unimpeded access to natural resources despite inherent deleterious impacts on the earth. Similarly, statutes prohibiting the pollution of waterways are weakened, if not abolished, in some instances. Upsetting the natural cycles and regenerating processes of nature kills the environment. Because the ecosystem is interconnected, human beings' physical relation to and aesthetic appreciation of the plant, animal, water, and air dimension of creation are impaired. The destruction of nature leads to increased morbidity and mortality of the human population.

Deregulation also fosters an environment of a free market that directly impacts workers' jobs, income, and family security, all for the interest of monopolized businesses. One of the reasons U.S. monopolies transfer operations to Third World countries is because trade unions are weak or nonexistent. When workers who produce the profits cannot offer a viable opposition, profits are guaranteed to flow directly to the owners of transnational monopolies. Furthermore, without bargaining power or protection for the profits they make, rural and urban workers suffer the threat of job loss, real declining income, and family instability. Lack of adequate income connects with health deregulation. Specifically, Third World governments relax food quality restrictions, control on the standards of medicines, monitoring of toxicity levels in drinking water, and any mandatory physical examinations for the populace, particularly infants and children. Without sufficient income, working people are incapable of satisfying health needs that, due to privatization, are now in the hands of the business sector.

Moreover, deregulation undercuts the function of the state. A transnational monopoly business from the United States enters a developing country and offers to invest if the state will loosen tax codes. These codes were originally established to do at least three things. One was to protect local businesses from being totally undercut by foreign investors. If these investors paid taxes, then that would, to a degree, take away from some money that foreign businesses could use to underprice local goods. With more money, foreign businesses are less pressed to raise prices on their products. They are able to maintain lower prices long enough until they run local manufacturers out of business. Second, taxes were initially put into place to prevent monopoly capitalists from repatriating 100 percent of their investments, thus leaving local citizens with no real benefits from the profits that the local government had permitted the foreign company to extract. And third, the local political machinery uses tax income to provide welfare benefits for the indigenous population. Without tax income, no money is available for these benefits. Actually, this function of the state became moot with neoliberalism's doctrine of privatization. In sum, deregulation in neoliberalism theology promotes a theological justification that supports the abolition of diverse forms of government regulation of the market and of capital ownership and distribution.

Third World leaders who oppose the theology of neoliberalism's three-prong approach of free market, privatization, and deregulation point to the particular harm developing countries have experienced. In the Third World, most people live in rural areas. Agriculture proves the key to any hope and vision of achieving sustainable development. Yet rural areas are where profound undermining of potential growth occurs. For instance, in Asia, forests and agricultural lands are being depleted and destroyed. "Steel bars and iron poles for factories are replacing trees; golf courses and plush residential areas are taking the place of rice fields, and other forms of technologies employed in newly-built industries prove to be destructive to all forms of life."[9] Even if developing countries reach for the promise of finance capital, they would have to rely heavily on the agricultural sphere. But in this sector is where the gospel of globalization subverts the potential growth of agriculture.

The doctrine of neoliberalism is the explanatory arm of the god of concentrated monopoly finance wealth. It says that one partakes of the grace of this god by offering unhindered access to further wealth concentration. Then Third World peoples will experience a "trickle-down" effect from the good works of transnational monopolies.

THE REVELATION OF GOD IN GLOBALIZATION

All religions posit some god, a force greater than any one human being. God surpasses the ability of one person, place, or thing to contain it. The potency of god compels its disciples to have faith that this god will be with them and will help them to enjoy the benefits that god's grace offers. Even after devotees of the religion die, the god continues to live. In this sense, god is absolute transcendence. At the same time, this god reveals itself through concrete manifestations to its believers and followers. Revelation enables the adherents to know that this god is real, has power, and yields results. The priests in globalization (e.g., the small group of families with disproportionate private ownership and distribution power of the world's wealth) and those who accept the leadership of the authority of this "clergy" act as if concentrated monopoly financial wealth is a god. And its revelation appears in definite economic, political, and cultural unveilings that disclose and award further opportunities for a concentration of monopolized wealth. The transcendent god reveals itself in immanent processes.

Globalization is a religious system of financial concentration on a global scale, rapidly pursuing its object of faith—an indefinite increased concentration. The religion of globalization is made up of a god, a faith, religious leadership, a trinity of religious institutions, a theological anthropology, values, and a theology. As a system, it makes no distinction between a sacred or secular sphere; it is all-pervasive.

Regarding its economic revelation, globalization pursues the integration of all markets throughout the world. One of its chief ethical practices is to lock developing countries into a dependent state by advancing loans and making these countries go into debt. As mentioned previously, loan advances from transnational monopoly businesses come with specific strings attached. The primary requirement is a free market—the ability of finance capital to penetrate the domestic economy of the debtor nation. This quick influx of investment can (after accumulating profit) just as easily exit a country and therefore disrupt the local financial arrangements and currency values. As a result, gross unemployment and mega-downsizing occur.

Debt repayment imbalances and the volatility of investments affect domestic Third World economies in an adverse manner. Developments in the agricultural sector do not benefit the majority of the country— working people in rural areas. Developing countries gear their domestic resources toward the export needs of the U.S. These countries shift from production for domestic consumption to cash crops for export. And so the majority of the populace suffer undernutrition, malnutrition, and, in extreme cases, starvation. Investment and saving strategies follow the immediate and long-range projections of multinational businesses. Local business markets, consumption habits, and production goals mirror the profit desires of the world's corporate giants.

Moreover, an unequal exchange exists in the export industries. To receive loans, countries must not only gear local resources to the international market; the export products cannot receive any subsidies from local governments. Goods, therefore, enter the global market and have to compete with similar products produced by multinational monopolies that can be deliberately underprice goods. Consequently while global monopoly business forces free market conditions on developing countries, America and other developed capitalist governments establish exclusive markets—a wall of protection against select Third World products. Protective legislation includes tariffs, quotas, and most-favored-nation (MFN) status. A globalized free market means a carte blanche for the flow of monopoly finance capital into Third World arenas and restricted freedom of export to monopoly financial centers from Third World countries.

An additional feature of globalization is the "new pattern of global division of labor with different countries specializing in the production of components of a single product like the motor car. This results in the increased movement of goods from one country to another, but within units of the same" monopoly capitalist institution.[10] Such a pattern slows down or makes impossible effective trade union organizing for the rights of local workers. Workers do not see the assembled finished product created by their labor, thereby adding to their disinterest in their jobs and in the process of production. Lack of interest can impact the desire to resist economic injustices. And because parts of a car, for example, are manufactured in different locations throughout the Third World, it is pretty much impossible to call for a worldwide strike against a globalized automobile industry. Using various countries as part of the international production division of labor throws off balance employees' attempts at raising wages, therefore leading to increased economic hardship.

Moreover, globalization brings on the ritual sequence of forced devaluation of local currencies, which gives rise to the printing of more money to pay for interest on debt and other needs of foreign investors. The printing of money induces hyperinflation, which exacerbates problems with purchasing power, which leads to increased dependency on jobs provided by foreign industries. In austere situations, purchasing power is further compromised when international lending institutions demand that caps be placed on wages as another precondition for financial and capital investment. From both the pricing and income sides, the ritual of the religion of globalization positions workers in a defensive economic posture.

The intensification of worldwide finance capital mobility creates an unprecedented movement of people across geographic boundaries. The phenomenon of worker migration has become a permanent feature of the earth. The relocation of transnational firms in rural areas tends to displace peasants, rural labor, and small farmers who, in turn, travel to cities and quasi-urban areas. The intense pressures of a tight and unfavorable job market in cities push urban workers to cross national borders into neighboring and distant Third World countries. The fortunate few travel to the United States and other developed capitalist centers for employment. The system of globalization offers a push-and-pull dynamic that feeds the economic hardships of the poor and working poor as well as their dreams of a better life for themselves and their children.

Finally, the economic revelation of the religion of globalization is enhanced greatly by time/space compression brought about by computer technological and telecommunication advances. Time/space compression allows instantaneous international activity of concentrated monopoly finance capitalist wealth. This god travels the world (thus is transcendent) with a literal press of a computer button. It never sleeps as the priests and their representatives of the religion trade and invest twenty-four hours a day (again, another mark of transcendence). The reality of time/space means that the literal time normally prescribed by the distance between areas no longer holds. In earlier times, capital and business transactions took place within a small town or village. People walked, rode horses, and later drove their cars to a bank or an investment center. Human beings actually met face to face, especially to physically examine investment possibilities prior to decision making.

With the advent of cyberspace and computer technology, monopoly finance capitalist wealth moves at the speed of light and compresses the travel distance required earlier by separate locations. The god of the religion of globalization defies all parameters. Commodity exchange, investment deals, and profit mobility occur instantaneously everywhere and anywhere. Within an instant via computer, e-mail, the

Web, or cell phone, the priests of globalization can conduct business in Cape Town, Tenerife, Rio, Sri Lanka, and Honolulu. If "people in Tokyo can experience the same thing at the same time as others in Helsinki, say a business transaction or a media event, then they in effect live in the same place, space has been annihilated by time compression."[11] The annihilation of space indicates the further supernatural strength of the god of the religion of globalization because it cannot be restrained by various confines of the natural, material reality.

Politics, a second revelation in the system of the religion of globalization, concerns how the god of increased monopoly wealth weakens the sovereignty and decision-making powers of local states, particularly in Third World nations. Globalization redefines the state. As indicated previously, as part of the initiation into the global dynamic, governments of developing countries make policy not for the benefit of labor, the environment, the domestic economy, or the marginalized sectors of society but in the interest of what will facilitate intensified wealth concentration.

On the world stage, corporate financial institutions make national borders illegitimate. The classic definition of a nation-state, which arose with the birth of European capitalism from the sixteenth to the eighteenth centuries, has become obsolete. Admission into globalization requires governments in developing countries to surrender most pretenses of serving as a safety net for the local public's welfare. To facilitate political stability among their own citizens, the state bureaucracies of developing countries act to squash any antiforeign organizations, leaders, and progressive sentiments.

The state does not become obsolete. It reconfigures its past functions—which were geared to the thriving of its own citizens—into a quasi-standing committee or outpost rendering services for transnational corporations. The state abdicates its former obligations to the common public good in areas such as health, welfare, and education. Privatization, including multinational businesses, becomes the deliverer of social services for a price.

In addition, the state, deploying its political clout, works as a leverage for corporate accumulation of wealth. It can allow transnationals the privilege of paying no or small real estate taxes. It permits these businesses freedom from sales taxes and income taxes for a set period of time. Sometimes municipal authorities provide free water and sewer lines and offer discounts on utility bills. Similarly, they gratuitously offer free landscaping of buildings and factories. The state, moreover, grants businesses the "right" to not pay taxes on investment income. Therefore, the state functions as a welfare agency for corporate wealth accumulation.[12]

As a result of the system of the religion of globalization, new goals and content emerge for the state. The concept of an independent, free-standing nation-state, negotiating the considerations of contained national interests of its citizenry, becomes moot. The state apparatus is pulled by and into the exigencies of globalization. In this sense, it lacks power. On the other hand, it still commands the reins of discipline and punishment for any recalcitrant citizens daring to cause an unstable environment for transnational investments. The state accepts the task of making, monitoring, and managing its own people as outlaws.

The political implications of globalization not only reveal themselves in the transformed politics of Third World states; likewise a new type of politics impacts the definition of place, location, and geography within other regions and nations. More exactly, the power dynamics and administrative resources begin to play out differently in the major cities that house concentrated business transactions. Just as nation-states are no longer what they used to be, so the major metropolises of the earth have become global cities.

National and global markets as well as globally integrated operations require central places where the work of globalization gets done. Further, information industries require a vast physical infrastructure containing strategic nodes with hyperconcentrations of facilities. Finally, even the most advanced information industries have a work process—that is, a complex of workers, machines, and buildings that are more placebound than the imagery of an information economy suggests. . . . Global cities are centers for the servicing and financing of international trade, investment, and headquarter operations.[13]

Finally, the politics of democracy on a world stage are made in the image of the god of globalization. Everything that this god touches has the potential of becoming its disciple for the furtherance of intensified monopoly finance capitalist wealth. To date, globalization is the highest form of capitalist democracy, a top-down democracy imposed against the benefit of the majority. Democracy, in the discourse of American civil society, suggests the right of all citizens to make decisions by exercising the franchise. And, in the common sense of American civic responsibility, because the United States has the highest form of democracy, such a political system of social relations among citizens needs to be exported over the entire earth. Yet the politics of real American democracy, as evidenced in its imposition throughout the world, include a power differential. Governments "elected" by their own people receive the rewards of being the friend of the free market as long as they serve the religion of globalization. In this scenario, state leaders appear to be elected by the majority vote of its populace, but in effect powerful "votes" of global finance capital sway domestic policymaking priorities. For governments exist at the decision and pleasure of transnational deliberations. "In other words, decisions [come] to be made on a transnational basis—a transfer of political power from the 'debtor' nation states to international agencies."[14] This new form of democracy inverts true democracy; people's power is replaced by elite finance capitalist power. And this latter unveiling of power does not even trickle down to the people. In fact, the structure of power has been transformed by capitalist liberal democracy and the freedom of the market.

In addition to offering an economical and political disclosure of itself, the god of concentrated monopoly finance capitalist wealth reveals itself by creating a recognizable culture in the world arena. It attempts to forge a popular cultural consensus and a popular lifestyle. Television serves as a major pioneer in developing a common way of being and worldview. It is not unusual, for instance, to discover destitute black South Africans in local townships addicted to daily showings of daytime, semipornographic soap operas from the United States. Crowded into one small room, many viewers are more conversant in the politics, economics, families, personalities, and dreams of these fictional characters than they are of the complexities of their own real country. Such visual pop art for mass international consumption not only creates an illusion about what American societies are actually like, it stimulates the imagination of the Third World voyeur into what he or she or the ideal should be. The vision of what is real and ideal, hopes and failures, often can be more powerful in molding a popular opinion than massaging aspirations to become something a viewer knows he or she will never be. Rural, semi-rural, or urban slum dwellers in the Third World might be stimulated to desire a trip to the United States or to imitate all that is seen on the television screen. Yet their real circumstances testify to the unlikelihood of becoming Americans. However, television soap operas and evening TV series spark people to think of ways to imitate and incorporate the visual lessons from fictional people into their own cultural trappings. People might wear their own native dress but styled like their favorite daytime TV star, for example. One does not have to live in America to be American; one can imitate America and become a hybrid international "citizen" at home.

Global cultural beachheads also manifest in the great television trio of MTV, CNN, and ESPN. If one is an American who travels throughout the world from hotel to hotel and from one home to another home (in both the Third World and the Second [European] World), one can literally feel a sense of knowing and experience a degree of familiarity by hearing MTV videos, observing the up-to-the-minute news of CNN, and catching the latest American sports tournaments within twenty-four hours on ESPN. These three media convey a desired reality on several levels. Music entertainment markets aesthetics to diverse age groups within a country. It differentiates lifestyles for focused groups. However, the impact of MTV does not cease once viewers leave the television area of their home or hotel. On the contrary, MTV operates as a public relations link in a chain of the entertainment market. What is seen on MTV can be purchased for listening pleasure from the local record shop. Similarly, MTV megastars are constantly on global concert tours. Via their private airplanes, they descend from the heavens and are already equipped with prefabricated road shows that do not have to be dovetailed to local environments. And t-shirts, cups, balloons, written literature, and related paraphernalia blanket the global concert venue like natural precipitation.

CNN presents the norms for worldwide crime, government, health, business, beauty, and other forms of human titillation and arousal. Whether broadcast from Atlanta or New York, CNN gives watchers in developing countries the notions of what is worthy and humanly normal material to be reported on. The monopoly capitalist owners of CNN allow and portray only certain types of crimes and human interest news items. What the globe perceives might not be what the globe approves of. But because everyone is seeing the same types of news items, then those items become normal. And more and more, news persons adopt the image of movie stars, and anchorpeople look more and more like male and female models. Furthermore, they no longer present news in a straightforward manner (à la the Walter Cronkite era). Now interpersonal banter is interspersed between hard news reportage. Similarly, some news reporters become superstars themselves. Viewers follow them regularly as they cover the volatile hot spots all over the globe. Usually backgrounded by heat-seeking missiles in the night sky or surrounded by a sea of bone-thin hungry children, the elite globetrotters and megastars of CNN become human interest stories within the news topics that they are covering.

ESPN offers the ultimate sports entertainment panorama. It uses far-away fishing junkets to showcase exotic places. It has the potential to instigate, aggravate, and manipulate relations between Third World countries, especially with nuanced portrayal of soccer matches. The triumphant hoopla of U.S. basketball heroes makes a legend out of America. Similar to the role MTV plays for the world tours of entertainers, ESPN helps to market merchandise. During the heyday of the Michael Jordan, Chicago Bulls era, team insignia could be found even in remote areas of Tibet.

Further intricate unfoldings of the cultural revelation of the religion of globalization appear with the McDonaldization of the world, closely pursued by KFC and Burger King. What these fast food monopoly capitalist corporations have in common with Pepsi and Coca Cola is the refined art of creating and altering the food tastes of the indigenous populations in developing countries. They effect a smooth strategy. U.S. soft drink monopolies undercut the prices of locally brewed soda pop, purchase a monopoly on the coin soda dispensing machines in a country, and flood the market with massive advertising linking their product with youth, sex, sports, and happy faces. Transnationals often give away free samples of cigarettes for a certain period of time. Once a significant segment of the people become addicted to nicotine, acts of gratuity revert to the normal acts of sales and purchase.

> Globalization has become the vehicle of cultural invasion. Technology is power. It becomes the carrier to those systems and ideologies (values and cultures) within which it has been nurtured. The tendency is to create a mono-culture. By mono-culture we mean the undermining of economic, cultural and ecological diversity, the nearly universal acceptance of a technological culture as developed in the West and the adoption of its inherent values. The indigenous culture and its potential for human development are vastly ignored. The tendency is to accept efficiency with productivity without any concern for compassion or justice.[15]

Culture is an industry inventing and spreading aesthetic sensibilities, fantasy imagination, the pursuit of pleasure, and compassion creation on a global scale. In addition to the financial institutions of culture cited so far, clothing, the Hard Rock Café, Planet Hollywood restaurant, pizza, pornography, alcohol, and the Hollywood film industry monopolies aid the god of the religion of globalization to remake the world in its own image. In the cultural industry, mergers and recombinations of satellite, television, cable, software, and broadcasting companies serve to circulate this god throughout every possible nook and cranny in the world theater.

PART FOUR

THE
CHALLENGE
OF THE FUTURE

CHAPTER SEVEN

James H. Cone and Thoughts for a New Generation

What is it that helps an individual or compels a scholar to keep energy and focus on one theme—the empowerment of the poor—since 1968? James H. Cone is such a person. Because of his response to his vocation and his mission to create a new academic discipline as well as maintain a lifestyle of intellectual discipline, Cone continues to lead the movement of liberation theologies into the new millennium.

Various thinkers and authorities on black sacred life were very creative in the middle to late 1960s as black theology was established. During this period, African American clergy, church administrators, and professors gave complete and selfless contributions to a new intellectual discipline for the black church and, in fact, for all justice-loving people. They refocused the vision of faith and the purpose of human life, and, as a result, they started the tradition of a new body of knowledge called black theology of liberation. But with the publication of his 1969 book, *Black Theology and Black Power,* and the stream of books after that, Cone has been called the father of black theology in the United States as well as in the world.

When black theology began, at stake was the right of and the necessity for black folk to think critically about the nature of their faith and their relation to God. Was there anything particular and positive about black sacred life? Did African Americans have a black theology— a conscious questioning about their faith and their actions? More specifically, could one be a black person and still be a Christian, or must one remain a "Negro" in order to be a believer in and follower of Jesus Christ? What was the content of the good news of Jesus? Did the thought and practice of the African American poor have a unique connection or any relationship at all with Jesus?

Cone, representing the first generation of black theologians, answered these questions emphatically. The content of the gospel of Jesus is the liberation, full humanity, and practice of freedom for the economically poor, the broken-hearted, and the vulnerable on earth. Following gospel writings in the Christian scripture, Cone claimed that Jesus was partial toward the poor because they had the least stake in holding on to their status and, therefore, were more open to Jesus' message of radical change. However, there is nothing inherently sacred in being black or being poor. In fact, Jesus still sided with these "little ones" of society by affirming the simple fact that they were human beings, despite times of their own self-inflicted problems. With this affirmation, Jesus offered a future promise to remove barriers such as racial exclusion or economic disparities in order to help free them from the mundane stress over fundamental survival issues as shelter, clothing, and food. With these essential necessities ensured, they could then dream about other ways of living as human beings. In contrast, the possibilities for the rich to enter the kingdom of heaven were so slim because they gave their ultimate faith and final commitment to their limited racial perspective and material possessions they owned. They would not follow Jesus because he was second to their ultimate allegiance to their social privileges and ways of living.

For instance, in the United States, Cone argued, too many of the white populace were Christians as along as they controlled and occupied the vast majority of positions of power within Christianity. White privilege defined their faith and practice. Most white Christians utilized their particular culture and view of the world as norms to judge everyone's religious thinking and faith-based practices. Creative sources from other traditions, divergent scholarship, and contemporary customs were sidelined or not taken seriously. This exclusive approach to theology and life had the effect of narrowing the contributions of generations of nonwhite citizens. The contrasting approach would have perceived all American experiences as fertile ground and scholarly possibilities for what determined the common good. Therefore, in his books, Cone concluded that "white theology" and the white church were compatible primarily with the elites. But this same white theology and church were not in sync with Jesus Christ and the Christian religion of right relations among people and with the rest of creation. If the dominant theology and churches were compatible with this Jesus story, then powerful white groups would not be monopolizing positions of power and the best that society had to offer in faith institutions, educational systems, and the broader civic arena. The perpetual narrative in the United States seems to present a story of racial exclusion in contrast to Jesus' good news for the broad spectrum at the bottom of the country. Instead of following the values of Jesus, for Cone, whites of religious faith had one aim: to maintain white power by any means necessary. And religious thought served as a crucial justification in this process.

To give evidence for this claim, Cone pointed out the contradiction between what white churches advocated in their creed and doctrines and what they witnessed to in their ethics and moral practices. It was easy for people to share communion together, participate in the same liturgy or church program, pray together on their knees or with heads bowed, and sing sacred songs together. But when all of the talking was over, why was it that the majority population still had power? It was not only a question of correct talk but a question of correct practice. It was a question of not only appreciating what people said but also measuring deeds in accordance with professed beliefs.

Because disproportionate white power dominated social relations in America, the particular black theology developed by Cone called on Christianity to be correct practice on earth as it is in heaven. This meant that Christianity—in contrast to what he called the heresy of white theology—urged human beings to have faith that Jesus would come again to bring about a social and spiritual revolution on earth. This future ideal of new social models should not capitulate to calls to be "realistic" and only accept token and partial victories. Christians were to work with the spirit of Jesus to bring about this complete rearrangement of the human society. Consequently, the initial negative emotional attacks against black theology came from the overwhelming majority of white theologians and church pastors as well as some black church leaders, because black theology touched the jugular vein of Christianity in America: the belief and practice that whites and the rich were the norm for Christianity.

By focusing on the locked-out voices in the African American community, black theology stretches out its vision to all poor and marginalized peoples. By structurally changing the systems that cause hurt, pain, and limited opportunities for the vulnerable of our citizens, the nation has the possibility of equalizing the best resources available. In this way, all people in the human family could enjoy mutual ownership and the benefits of the gifts for self-enhancement created by God for all to share together without privileges for elite families or individuals from any race or ethnicity.

Cone opened up a conversation about the critical and self-reflective nature of Christian theology. Likewise his writings presented an ongoing constructive and affirming theology intentionally rooted in the ground-swell of many different African American schools of thought and traditions, such as church, music, storytelling, political movements, individual thinkers, among other black perspectives. Given this brief backdrop, I'd like to suggest some challenges that James H. Cone's legacy presents to the second generation of black theologians.

CHALLENGES FOR THE SECOND GENERATION

From its origin in 1966 to the early 1980s, contemporary black theology developed under the bold leadership of the first generation of pastors and intellectuals. These older scholars literally had to fight for the right of the African American church and community to think theologically, to engage in their own systematic approach to and criticism of faith statements. Before the National Committee of Negro Churchmen (1966) and James H. Cone's *Black Theology and Black Power* (1969), the connection of black religious experience with serious intellectual implications for all of society was considered comic relief if not ignored by the white mainstream. Likewise the mushrooming civil rights and black power movements of the 1960s had not made a decisive break with the European-centered reflections of the dominant, mainstream theology. Although these intellectual and practical move-ments proclaimed a stand with black people, they failed to connect in a disciplined and consistent way the positive perspectives of Christian-ity to the "secular" cry for justice.

In some cases, black theologians had to slice through one-sided white religious and academic language and remind black churches of the liberation role of the gospel and the historic prophetic tradition in black people's history of faith and practice from West Africa until today. For the creators of black theology, the main issue was the Christian gospel of freedom for the poor. Consequently, the first generation used a passionate intellect that laid the foundation for all African American religious thought since the late 1960s. The overarching historic significance of the first generation is that it fought successfully for the right of black theology to exist and built it as a permanent, Christian and prophetic movement in the United States with influence throughout the world. Such a feat facilitated a serious discussion concerning the scholarly necessity for black religious thinking in the universal common good.

From the 1980s until the present, younger African American scholars have branched out into a variety of black theological concerns. While they seek to further the first generation's pioneering agenda, they also claim their own distinct approaches. Thus, these second-generation theologians are both heirs to and distinct from contemporary black theological founders. But unlike the older black scholars who worked primarily from outside the mainstream and were connected to a larger social movement, younger scholars are part of the status quo and operate as individuals.

DANGERS IN THE CASTLE OF THE MAINSTREAM

The second generation has greater access to support and resources inside and outside of religious institutions. Due to successful work of the first generation, younger scholars have been able to move closer to the mainstream and are more accepted. While they have inherited the accomplishments of the founding generations and a moral obligation to extend and deepen constructive analysis of the power of poor people in contemporary history, their closeness to the mainstream can seduce them into exclusive reliance on the experiences and opinions of white elite thinkers. Scholars of the current generation could become blinded by the accolades given for imitation of various models in dominant educational institutions. To succeed, they might feel pressured to dispense with black intellectual experiences of poor folk and insert African American examples into a European intellectual framework.

The second generation of black theologians can follow and fulfill their vocational responsibilities by using a mixture of interpretations. The recognition of multiple differences within the African American community is a positive move long overdue. Yet the important deepening of difference borders on a failure to perceive a vital unifying fact. Racial discrimination still permeates North American culture. Therefore, a crucial thread that must continue to tie together all areas of study and perspectives is a clear focus on working-class people and the poor. The overwhelming majority in the African American church and community fall within these categories. Are the lifestyles, commonsense wisdom, and gifts of these people central to all of theology? Are they to be investigated as mainstream theological sources and substantive concepts?

Furthermore, the Christian gospel's emphasis on the bottom of society likewise determines the vocational direction of black theology. Such a pro-poor position will also sharpen the distinctions between a "black theology of liberation" and a vague "black theology." The former encourages a gospel of good news for all of broken humanity, while the latter tends toward the maintenance of individual advancement and noncommunal privileges. The former fosters social change, the latter preserves the status quo in order for black middle-class representatives to enter. In all of its professional efforts, the second generation must ask whether it has tried to work for the interests of the African American poor. "Liberation" defines black theology because the sacred spirit of God and black ancestors focus on the practice of freedom for the marginalized of all societies. We must avoid an amorphous type of black theology that omits the crucial phrase of *liberation of the poor*. In ambiguity lies the danger.

Some second-generation black religious scholars have jettisoned not just liberation of the poor but the very category of black theology. This is troublesome because black theology was never created by an individual sitting in an ivory tower. Nor can it belong to one individual. Liberation is a gift from God to poor and working-class black folk. Black theology arose out of a spiritual and physical life-and-death situation for the bottom of African American communities as they accepted God's movement for justice. And this justice-making sought to foster the healing of the entire nation's soul as well as aid the voiceless in attaining a better material life.

Those who have dropped "liberation of the poor" from black theology or dispensed with the usage of "black theology" altogether are nearsighted. The current state of structural poverty means that the second generation (and all progressive people) are still engaged in a major effort and that there is still a positive vision that they try to help bring about on earth. But some are suffering from historical amnesia. Most African Americans who are in graduate education and other related positions of authority in the broader society are there because of those who preceded them—from West Africa, through slavery, legal and illegal segregation, antiblack racism, and through the civil rights and black power movements. In response to that prophetic tradition of creative resistance founded on love and justice, black theology answered the question of Jesus' relation to the movement of freedom of the black least in our midst. The failure to acknowledge, build on, or simply retell this tradition—without grasping the tradition's implications for the survival and service of black theology today—leads to negative consequences. Historical amnesia fosters a belief, conscious or unconscious, that black theology is simply another intellectual discipline of the educational establishment, a course that can be taken just like any other course.

In addition, the failure to maintain a clear vocational service and focus on a black theology of liberation for ignored voices comes from one's social location. Where do correct ideas come from? Do they fall from the sky? Most black religious scholars admit that social location greatly impacts their thinking. All black professionals who have "made it" in churches or the broad American mainstream are socially located in some form of authority position. A representative case in point are African American intellectuals. They include more black full professors, chairs of departments and committees, and graduate students than ever before. African American thinkers have more access to funding, publishing, speaking engagements, consulting opportunities, mentoring demands, travel opportunities, preaching schedules, books and articles available, conferences held and institutions built, and ties to the church than any other generation of black intellectuals in the history of the United States of America.

But entering the "castle" of the mainstream and being faithful to a gospel of liberation can present damaging possibilities. Those who take seriously African American thought as central to constructing a theology risk losing all the privileges gained in the castle when they persist in using the phrase "black theology" and, more specifically, "black theology of liberation of the poor." The reason is that the more opportunities they have, the more the pressure arises from structural authority to blunt an accent on liberation of social relationships on earth. From the perspective of the status quo, it could be much better to domesticate, tame, and legitimize black religious studies. This position undercuts any prophetic challenge to the monopolization of material resources and decision-making privileges and could limit the analysis for developing a comprehensive black theology today.

The fact that social location of today's black professionals has hindered the growth of black theology of liberation for the poor is understandable. In the 1950s and 1960s, the efforts of the masses of black people focused on letting more African Americans into the mainstream. Now that black professionals and the middle class are "in" institutions for the privileged, too many rely too much on individual know-how and loosen ties to their collective cultural wisdom. Moreover, they are pressured by the demands of professional and middle class culture. The subtle and not-so-subtle demands of social location impact how they relate to the plumb line of social justice. For example, social environments that privilege European-focused thought can influence what African American religious scholars publish on black theology of liberation.

Also, dropping black theology of liberation as a category is one easy way to sidestep the vocation to challenge the narrow and intense concentration of political, economic, and intellectual privileges in the United States and, in fact, the world. Monopolized wealth is one of the primary targets of the gospel for social justice. The material monopolization of God's gifts to all of humanity is a major condition for the vast poverty and economic inequalities in North America and around the globe. A black theology of liberation is one way of reminding all Americans that the good news gospel is about justice: healing the spiritually wounded and offering a new world to the physically broken.

Within the castle of the mainstream, another challenge for the second generation of black theologians is to keep the vocation of intellectual work as a service to the church and the community. Intellectual work is a spiritual calling and is another form of ministry. In the black church, family, and overall community, the complexities of the contemporary period of permanent unemployment, AIDS, violence, drugs, self-hatred and despair, domestic violence, psychological anxieties, the existence of one monopoly capitalist superpower, the increasing "feminization of black poverty," examples of positive resistance on the local and national levels, the reality of affirming and stable black families and black churches, and a host of other favorable and adverse questions require not less but more rigorous scholarly work.

The church is one community that holds black religious scholars accountable to the liberation faith mandate in the gospel and in the African American tradition. The church also helps to nurture their growth. In fact, the crucial concerns of the church and the rigorous exchange of ideas in academic settings can complement each other. But most educational systems in the United States, particularly for full-time professors, pull them away from meaningful organized faith communities. Educational institutions try to perpetuate themselves. And like all groups, they have established methods to lure professors into academia. In this world, advancement and staying power depend on how well people give time to publishing, teaching, and serving the academic lifestyle. Unfortunately, academic institutions have not appreciated fully the rich experiences and accumulated wisdom within faith communities and the broader American public. Clearly part of the gap between black professors and the church pew results from a well-organized educational system that demands time. Still, African American theologians must maintain creative and critical relationships to the black church—whether in the forms of teaching and preaching in the church, being associate pastors, leading workshops and seminars, consulting, or regularly sharing ongoing academic work with laypeople. Faith organizations, especially the black church, can help scholars to both serve the poor and challenge the poor when they fall short of a gospel message calling on freedom and right relationships for all peoples.

Next, the second generation of black theologians must place liberation theology in conversations at different levels. One audience is the professional level—undergraduate and graduate levels. A second level is the pastoral—the black clergy situated in the heart of the African American community. And the third and largest audience comes from the masses of black communities and poor and working-class folk. It is at this level that black theology has to continually remind itself of its audience—their feelings, pains, goals, fights, language, and hopes. The challenge is to speak on three levels with an emphasis on the third audience within the African American church and community and, through them, to all Americans.

Consequently, black theologians need to write so their families, communities, and descendants can understand their roles as the power of the poor in history. Most graduate schools would have students follow the standard practice that labels the most indirect, obscure writing as the most profound. Unfortunately, with this style of communicating usually only the most formally educated can talk to and among themselves. Poor communities, on the other hand, are left wondering what happened to those nice young black folk who went off to remote environments of higher education. But when these same promising African Americans from the community bring back books they've written, hardly anyone in their families and churches can read them.

In addition, for the poor, language is more than a mere convenient form to carry content. Language itself is also content and substance. People's language reveals their faith, backgrounds, hopes, desires, and connection to community. Language tells poor people whether the writer comes out of their world or at least takes their world seriously. Language, therefore, serves as a window into the lifestyle and beliefs of the writer as well as the writer's relation to her or his audience. If most blacks in the African American communities and churches are to see themselves in the work of black scholars, then the writers, when they write, must see the poor. And so religious language is part of life and should help make unjust relationships just. Today the great majority of publications are not geared for mainstream African American churches and communities; they are aimed exclusively at the academy. However, theology requires multiple languages for multiple audiences.

Furthermore, the complexities facing the black community and church in the twenty-first century demand a more sophisticated theoretical framework. What structure of concepts can aid the liberation conclusions and practices of black theology? What insights might be taken from a host of academic disciplines and related experiences from liberation theologies in the Third World? What theories can help black theology move from its primary sources of the African American experiences to its theological conclusions about God's intention for oppressed humanity? For example, how do those concerned with black religion take interviews with ex-slaves or the rap music of black youth and jump to conclusions about what Jesus Christ is telling poor black folk to say and do? Theory can become a vital tool for clarity in the story of God's working with the black poor to move them from being passive victims of oppression to being active people searching for a more compassionate and just lifestyle for all of creation.

Women, too, continue to challenge the vocational tasks of the second generation of African American theologians. However, books and articles need to emphasize more the critical issues of most black women, the group consisting of black women who are poor, working class, unemployed, and/or single heads of household. How do we make their survival and full human dignity prominent in scholarship? Their day-to-day triple experiences of economic dislocation, gender oppression, and racial negativities can enrich the entire theological focus of black religious studies. The point where various types of intense human pain come together usually provides the most fertile grounds for creative and sustaining work as it relates to the God–human interaction.

In order to harness all of its strengths, the second generation will have to conduct a prolonged, organized conversation and joint practice between womanists and (male) black theologians. An encouraging model appears in *My Sister, My Brother: Womanist and Xodus God-Talk* written by the wife-and-husband team of Karen and Garth Baker-Fletcher. Their book begins the dialogue on God, Christ, humanity, the ancestors, the church, and the last things in Christian hope. A similar model is the ongoing course entitled "Womanist Theology and Black Theology" cotaught by my wife, Linda E. Thomas, and me at the Lutheran School of Theology at Chicago and the University of Chicago Divinity School. Using the disciplines of anthropology, systematic theology, political economy, and African American studies, we have womanist and black theologies converse around issues of race, gender, class, sexual orientation, and the ecology.

And the second generation needs to identify clearly the location of passions of resistance. What are poor people angry about today? For instance, does rap music provide any hints about the state of urban black youth and the destructive and constructive potential they offer the black church and community and, in fact, all of America? Where exactly is the black Christ today fighting beside the broken-hearted and leading a struggle for emancipation? Similarly, where are healthy and innovative, life-affirming testimonies in African American culture now? Securing responses to these questions requires the discipline of anthropology and its tools of long-term fieldwork and ethnographic studies of blacks today and tomorrow.

The historical foundation of African American religious life in North America demands rethinking of how to develop black theology today. The period of slavery—where black people were actually forged

into "African Americans" and the black church began to define itself—
and the 1950s and 1960s civil rights and black power movements in
particular offer a storehouse of traditions, lessons, cultural values, and
political strategies for today's African American community. What is in
the faith of enslaved black folk that provided the groundwork for survival
and liberation of black Americans even until today? What happened in
the 1950s and 1960s that caused the African American community to
feel a sense of collective self-worth and transformative values and inspired
a movement based on a liberation faith? The purpose of religious history
is to change the world today. Yet the effort to address unjust relationships
in the contemporary period grows out of a historical legacy of black and
white interactions. Since European Christians carried Africans into the
land of the Native Americans, millions of poor and illiterate black folk
have developed a proactive and enduring faith, a faith that has looked
into the eyes of life's absurdities and survived. Moreover, that faith has
ensured black positive cultural self-identity, political self-determination,
and spiritual renewal. These are profound lessons for enabling the growth
of the entire nation.

Finally, the second generation will have to build and show models
of basic Christian communities in local areas on the everyday level. Such
locations, whether centered around a particular church or household
meetings of African American Christians, would teach, preach, and
practice a black theology of liberation for all to see and hear. If there will
be third and fourth generations of black theology, then the second
generation will have to meet these challenges and more.

THE TWENTY-FIRST CENTURY

The second generation of African American theologians continues to
produce new scholarship to meet new challenges at the beginning of the

twenty-first century. At the crossroad of two millennia, they hear the painful but powerful voices of the state of black America and the cries of the unborn demanding to know what preparations are being made for the children-to-be. Basically, the second generation has to integrate a message of hope for a more just social order, a critical acceptance of African American religious history, and an understanding of theological, cultural, and political power in the United States today.

But blatant and subtle forces are attempting to negate formally trained intellectuals, the church, and the community from drawing on the potential of a new African American spirituality and thinking. This occurs when power holders in mainstream decision-making positions foster an ethos that undercuts creative explorations into the overflowing springs of black thought. On the other hand, younger scholars trip and fall when they fail to balance the basic prophetic and servant roles of black theology's vocation. In fact, black theology has a calling to organize itself at the service of silenced voices. African American theologians must listen to and help empower these voices and thereby themselves.

For those called to scholarly activity to broaden the conversation on behalf of the nonprivileged, educational settings of higher learning can provide a vibrant and crucial location for vigorous intellectual work. Institutional systems and colleagues who claim that the life of the mind can make a difference to the survival of real human beings in North American society offer a vast storehouse of knowledge. Within the academy, one of the major challenges for the second generation and all concerned about justice is fleshing out constructive conclusions by building comprehensive, positive, well-thought-out visions. In a sense, research and teaching provide one aspect of sacred space to press the limits of complex and substantive thinking in service to the greater human community.

However, at the same time, in black theology's servant role, it must shoulder prophetic and critical responsibilities. Not all black churches are preaching and practicing the Christian gospel of returning all of society's wealth to the poor; having a black preacher and black congregation could mean the propagation of an incorrect theology. Service to, love for, and affirmation of the poor and the entire church and the community mean keeping them accountable to what they have been called to say and do. Ultimately, moving into the twenty-first century, the vocation of the second generation of black theologians will help bring about God's new common wealth of justice on earth.

CHAPTER EIGHT

A New Common Wealth

The earlier chapters in this book have offered black theology as an intentional analysis of the nature of a spirituality, faith, or belief in the ultimate hope for a transformed humanity and society. As a self-critical and self-reflective theology—looking at the divine and human interaction—black theology draws on a host of resources and disciplines to provide both a vision of future possibilities and compassion for different voices silenced or ignored in our country and the world. For instance, the progressive tradition of the African American church calls on the healing of the soul, fostering of committed theological education, an engagement in a prophetic ministry to change the world, healthy and thriving families, and support for the full and equal standing of Africa and other Third World countries in the global arena.

Furthermore, black theology faces the human questions of daily life and points to the presence of a spirit of a just future brought about by a human effort based on freedom as a sacred lifestyle. True freedom manifests when each individual experiences in his or her heart and head that the soundness of one's humanity depends on compassionate concern for and persistent practice with those without privileges. In other words, the health of one's humanity hinges on the health of another. Similarly, black theology sees the realization of each person's calling as it serves the collective body. More specifically, the Jesus story presents a powerful paradigm for earthly equality among all, a democratic arrangement in collectivity, and the nurturing of individuality in relation to communal social relations. In this way, the conversation directs us to consider the broad contours of a new heaven and a new earth.

If human beings in the twenty-first century are to develop a positive faith, good values, and healthy relationships among all peoples, then the future of the black poor is key. The ongoing problem and the creative challenge of the twenty-first century will be greatly impacted by what happens to the African American poor. With this group in North American society, we discover the coming together of the racial and class foundations upon which the United States was built. Race continues to matter. It is, in fact, the ever-present spoken and unspoken text among race relations. Too often, race remains the easy scapegoat in a social system that allows the African American poor to become the brunt of sectors of the nation who need to vent their frustration on a group of citizens that deviates from the norm. Even under the false cover of objectivity or seeking the most qualified person, people with privileges and power make decisions based on race without mentioning the word. It is the fundamental hidden criterion in social interactions. Consequently, the soul of the United States will become whole when conversations about, clarity on, and corrections of race emerge as priorities in everyday North American culture.

In addition to race, African American workers undergo the vulnerable and creative realities of class. The income and livelihood of black working people depend not on owning and controlling wealth but on selling their skills, knowledge, and muscle to someone else who pays them an income. The power and wisdom of laboring folk remain the engine that has built the United States and supplies the pioneering energy for social, technological, and spiritual advancements today. The richness of race and class experiences of black working people offers profound lessons for the rest of the nation. How is it that this sector of society has endured since 1619? How has it been able not only to endure but to flourish? A large part of this response derives from their deep spiritual beliefs and the deep suffering they have encountered for no other reason than their color, an attribute given to them by God, and their laboring status, given to them by nonworking people. African Americans who work know what suffering is. And, as a result, they perhaps have the clearest perspective on how to help maintain other people's human dignity and full humanity without perpetual suffering. Black theology— the connection between a faith in liberation and oppressed black folk's instincts for liberation—responds to this problem and this challenge brought about by the intersection of race and class. Black theology continues to offer hope for all humanity. It consistently reminds us all that God has pointed us to a vibrant and wholesome community by learning from the experiences and leadership of black working people. That is why the black poor remain the plumb line for the twenty-first century's future.

Black theology means that Jesus still labors with the working poor as they attempt to be holistic human beings and reach their abundant humanity. For instance, whenever African American communities organize to love the positive dimensions of black culture and their rich African tradition and strive to enjoy all the resources on this earth, Jesus is with them. The ability of the oppressed to define themselves and to determine how the wealth of society will be used, based on a faith in freedom, is black theology. Black theology comes out of the particularity of the

African American church and other communities of faith that highlight the divine spirit of justice as a gift to diverse peoples of the world.

A NEW HEAVEN AND NEW EARTH

And this spirit, along with all poor and working people, has the goal of building a new common wealth on earth as it is in heaven. Under the guidance of God's spirit, to reach this new society means each person at the bottom of today's society will begin to exercise her or his own individual gifts given by God. At the same time, it means all of the poor will start to share collectively in the vast resources offered by God to everyone. The long-term effort to actualize the full humanity of poor black folk will help replace systems and forces of habit that concretely restrict justice for all of the poor. In this dynamic, when the most oppressed start to exercise their God-given humanity, they begin to make the rich accountable to the gospel that says that everyone ought to have equal stake at each level in society. The practice of freedom on the part of the least among us means that the structures that cause oppression will be changing. This change begins the process of eliminating poverty, which, from the Christian perspective, will not be removed completely until the second coming of Christ. Christ will usher in the fullness of the new common wealth. In this sense, the future social relations are "not yet." However, because Jesus was here on earth and made a historic difference in human lives by providing some alternative possibilities for how human beings can live together, the new common wealth is, in fact, "already" here. If it is a reality, then all human beings need to conduct ourselves as if we are living out the new now. This is the meaning and the miracle of the "already" and the "not yet."

The new common wealth is what some Christians call the "reign" of God or the "kingdom" of God. But the word "reign" sometimes suggests a ruler who does not bring freedom or work with his subjects. It can create the image of a despot or a patriarch who makes all decisions and the rest of the family simply carries out his rules and commands. Likewise the term "kingdom" can bring to mind the harmful rule of a king, a throwback to the Middle Ages in Europe as well as to the patriarchal structures during the time when Jesus walked the earth. In kingdoms, an individual male has the power and makes all the decisions; as a result, he holds ultimate authority over the rest of the kingdom.

Part of the reason black churches and most other people refer to "reign" and "kingdom" is because they accept uncritically the language of the King James' version of the Bible. But King James felt the king's English was the best and most refined language in the world. When King James of England did not like the current French translation of the Bible, he hired educated people to translate the Bible the way he wanted it to be translated. That is why we have the King James version of the Bible. The language of King James reflects the way people spoke English during the period when the king controlled the "reign" of his "kingdom" in seventeenth century England. But Jesus never spoke in the language of King James. Jesus actually spoke Aramaic. Therefore, we can utilize the substance of the good news and clothe it in other positive metaphors for new social interactions.

For instance, in contrast to "reign" and "kingdom," the phrase "new common wealth of God" paints a more just picture and a more liberated vision of our relation with God on earth as it is in heaven. Instead of a male patriarch who "reigns" in his "kingdom" over the rest of us like we were peasants from the Middle Ages, instead of a male, rich king who dominates the rest of his society, the new common wealth tells us that all of humanity will share in the best of God's creation.

Furthermore, from the perspective of the new common wealth, God exists among the poor—the world's majority—and works with them so that they might have the ability to name who they are and determine the distribution of the resources of the earth. Unlike the "reign" or the "kingdom," the new common wealth is a society where no one human being will rule over another and no one individual or group of families will own more than anyone else. What follows are some visions about the theological content of the common wealth. If Christianity is based on an incarnation where God's spirit really did mix with human flesh, then we need to say a word about how God's spirit will empower different parts of our human society.

ECONOMICS

Based on the Book of Isaiah (chapter 61), Jesus clearly states that the spirit from God had called him or anointed him for one purpose: to be with the poor of this earth and to announce good news to them. Who are the poor? They work everyday but do not own the corporations or businesses where they work. They are the ones who suffer from the neglect of those who have economic power in the nation. They are also the marginalized in society: the unemployed, the underemployed, poor women who are vulnerable to abuses of male privileges, poor blacks attacked by a culture that continually disregards their material prosperity and their spiritual dignity, poor lesbians and gays who are seen by society as polluted, and poor children and the elderly who are discarded by different communities.

But the spirit of liberation brings good news to all who are forced to the margins of the nation's vision. In the Book of Acts (chapter 2 and verses 44-45), we see what the new human community can become. "All whose faith had drawn them together held everything in common: they would sell their property and possessions and make a general distribution as the need of each required." The new common wealth, on the economic

level, will have all of society sharing the wealth of that society. God gave
creation for all of humanity. But a few individuals and a very small group
of families have monopolized the inheritance and distribution of these
resources. Here wealth is very different from income. Even when working
people earn an income, they still are subject to the profit decisions of the
people for whom they work because the employers privately own wealth.
Wealth determines income.

Therefore, the black poor and poverty for all of humanity will
disappear when the poor are no longer people whose only option is to
work for others and are forced to receive an income. Poverty will
disappear when the poor share in the abundance of wealth and break the
current global monopolization of the earth's resources, thereby bringing
about a democracy in economics. Again the Book of Acts (chapter 4 and
verses 32 and 34-35) helps us to understand this difference between
income and wealth.

> The heart of the multitude of believers was one and their soul was one,
> and not a single one said anything of what he had was his, but all things
> were in common. . . . There was no poor person among them, since
> whoever possessed fields or houses sold them, bore the proceeds of the
> sale and placed them at the feet of the apostles; and a distribution was
> made to each one in accordance with his needs.

The key to the economic common wealth is to foster a common
will, faith, and vision with the poor. To achieve this degree of clarity
and resolve, the bottom sectors of society will have to develop a lifestyle
in line with the purpose of the spirit of liberation. This spirit calls for
the majority of the world and, through them, the entire global
community to act as stewards: to accept the natural resources, human
potentialities, and technological knowledge as divine gifts. By growing

into the ultimate goal of this spirit of liberation, the poor then will be able eventually to realize new social relationships on earth in which everyone is on an equal level.

African American working people and the poor are part of the majority of the United States, which is a country filled with millions of people without wealth who are Christian and non-Christian, in the church and outside of the church. Those living in poverty, therefore, should participate in the stewardship and ownership of the major economic corporations and commercial businesses and wealth—the land, everything built on it, and scientific innovation. To carry out such a new democracy requires reallocation of current political economic structures toward sharing. As the beginning process to abolish poverty, black working people and poor folk should have a share in this ownership and decision making that is similar to their percentage of the population. Likewise, poor black women's share in this new type of stewardship should reflect their representation among the U.S. citizenry. To facilitate this process and spirit of liberation, major corporations and financial institutions would be owned collectively, not by an individual person or a small group of North American families. Moreover, the resources from these financial institutions would be used to help poor and working people to set up small and medium-size businesses in their communities as another form of collective participation and healthy renewal for the overall common good. Economic democracy, the ethics of this steward-ship, provides various ways of unleashing the creative potential of previously untapped people and ideas.

POLITICS

Because the majority of the U.S. population is made up of poor and working people, the elected officials (on national, regional, and local levels) should be chosen from among that group. The achievement of this goal would probably mark the first time in the nation's history where true political democracy—a group of elected officials who reflect the majority of the people in the country—existed to energize the passion of political ownership for all of the nation's constituents. The reason that this does not happen today is because now the first criterion to be elected in the United States is to own, control, and monopolize wealth or have access to resources and money. In contrast, in the democratic politics of the new common wealth where members of the majority are elected, the main criteria are that a person: (1) has to come from the majority population of working people and the poor; and (2) is willing to lead by serving others. There is no third criterion of needing wealth or lots of money.

Another important political part in the new common wealth is self-criticism and easy recall. Each public official would have to offer public self-criticism to the American people as one way of guarding against arrogance. Self-criticism means an open examination to determine if the elected official has carried out the instructions which were given by the people who elected her or him. It also would be a reminder that the elected official is not there for her- or himself but as a servant of poor and working people.

Easy recall allows citizens to remove politicians from office without going through a lot of bureaucracy. Public leadership would foster a culture of accountability and transparency. Any public official who lied, stole money, committed adultery or murder, misappropriated funds, and the like would be removed from office.

Black men and women, other people of color, and all women would hold public offices in numbers reflecting their percentages of the U.S. population. Out of such a diverse wisdom, experiences, and perspectives, the best political leadership can be forged representing all sectors and all walks of life. The broadest diversity yields an increase in developing ways of government amenable to each part of the country. Commitment to eradicating structures that position the majority of people at the bottom rung of the country would serve as the plumb line for all politicians.

RACE

The new common wealth will encourage the celebration of the cultural contributions of black poor folk. Poor and working-class African Americans have achieved much since Africans were first brought to the "New World." Intellectual contributions and other gifts in science, music, art, drama, dance, and so on need to be highlighted as part of the national culture. Another important part of racial affirmation is accepting and promoting how poor black folk have developed their own way of speaking English. In the new common wealth, there will not be what today is called "standard English," which is usually a code word for one dominant way of communicating in English. In the future, various ways of speaking English will be healthy for the common good. National, regional, and local resources that come from the common ownership of wealth would be used to promote black cultural and language contributions to the nation.

The new common wealth does not establish social relations where there is no celebration of particularity. Part of the new community is to support the African American poor and working people to explore further the richness of the racial characteristics that God has given them. It will truly be a new tradition when all people can say that black is beautiful and blackness becomes part of the norm of what it means to be a full human. No one racial culture and biological traits—nose and lip structures, hair texture, and skin color—will be "good" and others "bad." The clearest example of when "black is beautiful" materializes as an accepted positive value is when the majority of the African American community begins to love their natural black selves and stop trying to imitate white people. When black folk stop paying billions of their dollars to the hair and skin industries, black will become beautiful for them. The more they love themselves, the more others will love them.

GENDER

The new common wealth will allow poor black women to reach their full humanity despite their gender. Men will not occupy any roles automatically. Poor African American women will serve in the leadership roles and make major decisions in every section of the nation—business ownership, politics, education, religion, the family, and more.

For instance, women will have a say in the division of labor in household chores and raising children. This option to choose how they will function in their own household includes the option of hiring someone else to do all of these chores. Whichever option is chosen, whoever decides to perform household chores will receive one of the highest salaries among the different jobs in the nation. This is so because raising children should be the highest priority in any civilized society. The legacy and vigor of the future of the United States revolve around the grooming of the children as future heirs and trustees of the earth and human communities. The transformation of poor children out of structural poverty and into participants in the best knowledge, sports, leisure, travel, and self-esteem support mechanisms offered by a country shifts a vision away from individualistic profit accumulation to people on the underside of the nation. Moreover, Jesus called on children—the little ones—as an incarnation of his vision for a just society.

As women will be empowered in the home and the greater popula-tion, in the African American church, room will be made for black women to bring new styles of church leadership and to become pastors of black churches. If African American women make up to 70 percent of the congregations, then 70 percent of the black pastors should be women. This is church democracy.

Likewise, poor African American women—those on welfare, those who clean private homes and business establishments, those who are the backbone of institutions, those who work for others—will be transitioned into positions of owning wealth, businesses, corporations, and financial institutions. The nation and various other types of communities do not tap the leadership and intelligence of black women at the bottom of the society because we assume that they have no worth except for serving others. Perhaps the success of the new common wealth will depend on oppressed African American women reaching their highest potential. When society sees it as normal for these women to run institutions and make decisions and hold positions of national leadership, we will be closer to the new common wealth.

Moreover, gender in the new common wealth includes at least two more points. First, poor black women will have to learn to love themselves more. The more they take care of themselves and not be servants to or dependent on men, the more they will be able to develop more healthy relations. Most of the time it is assumed that whatever happens, the black woman (sister or daughter, but usually mother) will be there to take care of the situation or clean up after everyone else, or sacrifice herself in order for the rest of society to feel better. In the worst situation, African American women have had to play the role of the mule or work horse for the rest of the African American community and in the larger culture and labor force benefiting privileged white communities. So, in addition to having an equal share in the democratic economics of the nation's wealth and representation in politics, poor black women have to develop more values of self-love and independence. That comes about through recognition of and steadfast adherence to the spirit of liberation, which yields self-love and self-esteem.

Black men need to develop a new definition of what it means to have a male gender. In other words, what does it mean to be a healthy heterosexual African American man? Being a heterosexual man includes first of all recognizing all the privileges that African American men enjoy because of their male gender in contrast to both black women and the male gender of homosexual black men. To be a new man demands that we have to raise some hard questions. What do we do to and for our wives and girlfriends? How do we raise our children? What negative beliefs and practices do we bring into our families and homes that we get from the larger white society of cutthroat competition and the ideas that say men are superior to women and automatically the heads of their homes? How do we relieve stress and promote healthy spirituality?

How do we handle conflict, anger, forms of self-hatred, despair, joy, love, successes, faith, challenges and other rewards as they relate to being a black man in the United States? What male privileges do we have as black men? For instance, we need to confess how it is a privilege to not have to think about being raped; to point out how men get paid more than women for the same work; to admit that men (black and white) often discuss and agree on major decisions in settings where women are absent or are not allowed; to recognize that moral standards are applied more strictly to women than they are to men; to know that when we walk into a room (most of the time), we will be favored because we are male; to understand that usually what we say gets acknowledged in a group setting more often than when black women speak; to point out how car salesmen and auto mechanics usually try to take advantage of women more than men; and to think about not having to clutch our pocketbooks when a man passes us by.

There are several ways to develop a new black man. One is to show how it is a serious problem to call for the freedom of African American people while still keeping black women at the bottom of that group. How can the African American church and black theology and community preach and teach about a spirit of liberation while, at the same time, pressing black women down to the bottom? If the success of the church and theology is based on the situation of the black community, then that experience should include all people; the majority of that reality is women. For instance, all African American churches believe that the Bible stories of "slave obey your masters" are wrong. But these same churches will say that the other stories about "women obey your husbands" and "be submissive" apply to women. Black men have to recognize that the circumstances of our mothers, sisters, daughters, nieces, grandmothers, and aunts do not stop with race. They also have to deal with their female gender—what it means to be a woman or a girl.

Another way of approaching the creation of a new male gender is to learn from how black women live in this world. More African American men must focus only on the experiences of black women. In history, church, and today's society, what do black men learn from listening to, studying, and having conversations with African American women?

A third way is to be self-critical of what it means to be an African American man and develop positive models of the new manhood. The guiding rule here is that black men can reach their full humanity as creations of God only when black women also reach theirs. Men cannot be human until they accept the humanity of women. Consequently, if men oppress women, then those men are also oppressing themselves.

Ultimately to create a new male gender is to feel that God loves men and therefore men should love themselves. If we men feel that God loves us and we also love ourselves, we will not have to dominate women or anyone else. To dominate women is to deny God's love.

SEXUAL ORIENTATION

The new common wealth will have to come to terms with sexual orientation in the African American community and church. One of the greatest points of unity that black heterosexuals have is their agreement to oppress and discriminate against black lesbians and gays in the church, family, and larger society. Black heterosexuals have a privilege over black homosexuals. Although black heterosexuals suffer from class exploitation in economics, racial oppression relative to whites, and male supremacy especially for women, one of the few negative things heterosexuals can hold on to as a group is to oppress lesbians and gays. The tragedy of African American heterosexuals is that they continue a system of oppression using some of the same arguments that whites have used against blacks and men have used against women.

The Bible is brought into the conversation as a justification to oppress lesbians and gays. But it is a problem when African American churches state that the stories in the Bible are wrong when they call on slaves to obey your masters, and black heterosexual women argue that the passages proclaiming women should obey men are sinful. Yet this same Bible is interpreted as condemning homosexuals to hell without salvation unless they become heterosexuals. If it is wrong to interpret the Hebrew story and the Jesus narratives as instructing black slaves to obey white masters and women to obey men, then why isn't it wrong to interpret this same Bible as saying homosexuals should deny the sexual orientation that God gave them when God created them?

Others claim that it is not natural for two men or two women to love each other sexually. This argument, which uses nature, is similar to how white racists described blacks as unnatural people, claiming they are naturally inferior in their thinking. And it is natural for whites to own most of the resources and wealth, while it is natural for blacks always to be at the bottom of the job market. Heterosexuals say what is natural in society, because heterosexuals have the power and the privilege to define people who are different from them.

Some believe that homosexuality destroys the black family. But here again heterosexuals are defining the family in the traditional way of the patriarchal father married to the mother who has their children. The black community has always defined its own experience of being a family in the United States. Thus there is a tradition of creating new types of families different from the patriarchal legacy normalized in the dominant religious, educational, legal, and entertainment perspectives of the United States. In addition, nothing prevents homosexuals from having children and raising a family. Likewise, some of the most stable families in the black community are gay and lesbian families. The argument for a traditional patriarchal definition of the family covers up the many abusive heterosexual families where black men beat their wives, sexually abuse the women in the family, and are alcoholics and drug addicts. However, this is not to forget the thousands of healthy and exemplary black heterosexual families in the United States.

Creating positive human interactions between various sexual orientations likewise follows the ethics and vision of the spirit of liberation. That is to say, the new common wealth will have heterosexuals believing that their full humanity can be reached only when the full humanity of poor homosexuals is achieved. God has created all human beings and did not make a mistake. Divine love provides liberation for all humanity, and this includes poor black lesbians and gays.

CHILDREN AND THE ELDERLY

Regardless of race, class, gender, and sexual orientation, the success of the new common wealth will be judged by how well we treat the elderly and poor black children. To cherish the preciousness of God's creation for the future of humanity, all children would have access to free day care and free education from the first grade to graduate and postgraduate education. All children will have free healthcare and access to the best sports and cultural opportunities and facilities. All children would be able to travel and learn about the world and enjoy safe and healthy families, whether biological or extended. Perhaps the elimination of poverty among children and the status of poor children will be the main definition of whether the new common wealth is achieved. Any society that puts profit and making money before the well-being of its children is doomed to eventual failure.

Similarly, the elderly represent the wisdom and history of the black community. They embody the sacrifices that allowed their children and grandchildren to survive and "make a way out of no way." The elders are the natural leaders of the poor. When the elderly suffer, there is a break in ties to God, the ancestors, tradition, and knowledge—all needed for spiritual and social change.

EMOTIONAL AND PSYCHOLOGICAL HEALTH

On a personal level, full humanity in the new common wealth means a healing of personal wounds. Psychotherapy teaches us that we are all suffering as adults because of scars, wounds, and negative issues that have not been resolved from childhood experiences. This covers many problems—low self-esteem, sexual abuse of children, children of adult alcoholics, and different types of ways that we are addicted to being dependent on other people or other things. People cannot reach their full potential in relation to the community if these psychological and emotional "ghosts" continue to make them feel negative things about themselves and others.

If we do not pay attention to these negative feelings and actions, then we pass them on to our children, our wives, husbands, lovers, our colleagues at work, and others we come in contact with. Moreover, for those who have positions of power, the disease of childhood skeletons is projected on society and the world.

In other words, it is the wounded "children" within us who take over our adult bodies. And when these adult bodies have power and privilege, the wounded "children" within us can be deadly as they seek to make the world pay for the crimes committed against us when we were young. If we do not give adequate attention to correcting these abusive ways of seeing ourselves and interacting with others, these negative feelings will be passed on from one generation to the other. It is extremely difficult to be a productive human being when one walks around everyday filled with negative thoughts and feelings.

NATURE

The new society will, in addition, appreciate the importance of the earth. The more the human community interferes negatively in earth's normal cyclical functions, the more the natural resources humans need to survive on will die. If the earth and nature die, then all of humanity will die. Therefore, black theology will have to develop a theology of nature or ecology, not only because all people are contributing to the death of nature, but because the particular survival of African American people is at stake. For instance, most dump sites in America are found in or very near black and Latino/Hispanic working-class populations. Therefore, a black theology of liberation for nature is a political issue. Those in society with power and wealth cause most of the pollution and waste. Yet they dump this waste and pollution in poor black and brown communities.

We have to love and care for nature or the ecology because God has created it. And God has created humans to take care of nature. This does not give us permission to dominate and exploit and abuse all of creation that are not human beings: plants, animals, air, water, fire, land, and so forth. The earth is sacred and it is a gift to humanity.

THE THIRD WORLD

Finally, the new common wealth will connect the black poor with the poor in Africa, Asia, the Caribbean, Latin America, the Pacific Islands, and North America. African American people are not isolated in these times of global relationships. The world's poor need to be in conversation in order to figure how it is that they became poor. Despite differences in language and culture, there are many similarities. Full humanity for the bottom of society can be a common theme to discuss and a common goal to reach. How can the world's working people and poor move to positions of sharing in the wealth and resources in their own countries? How can black, indigenous peoples, women, and other oppressed peoples become free throughout the globe? How can the universal poor, the majority of the earth, work together and share the benefits of their knowledge, cultures, and wealth? How can Christians, Muslims, Buddhists, African indigenous religions, Shintoists, Shamanists, Taoists, Confusionists, Jainists, Hindus, Jews, and others come together based on a belief in and practice of liberation of the poor?

SOME FINAL THOUGHTS FOR THE FUTURE

The future of black theology of liberation depends on how this new common wealth is brought about with the divine spirit of liberation in the twenty-first century. It is a vision of a future society that includes a very complex form of liberation and full humanity. It depends on uplifting the status of working people and the poor. If it is an issue dealing with race, gender, class, sexual orientation, nature, or the global situation, the first question is: how are the church and other communities of faith relating to the least in society?

Why focus on the poor? The focus on the poor does not suggest that black poor and working-class folk do not suffer from psychological and physical abuses, arrogance and self-hatred, destruction of the environment, patriarchy and homophobia, careerism and self-centered individualism, and other issues. A black theology of liberation judges all people by one test: Do they side with God's work to liberate the poor and working-class people of all colors and ethnicities and bring in a new common wealth? Whenever poor and working-class folk go against their own interests, and as coworkers with God for freedom, then they are wrong and have to be opposed. Poverty in and of itself is not sacred.

A black theology of liberation sides with the poor because the spirit of liberation has already opted for the poor. The poor sections of our community are chosen by God—and for Christians, through Jesus Christ—because they suffer from being at the bottom of the country in terms of not owning any wealth; being objects of racial, gender, and sexual orientation discriminations; and being entrapped by a host of psychological addictions. Because they are the majority of society and the world, when they are free and able to be full human beings, they provide a more favorable condition to alter nondemocratic structures experienced by the rest of the world. This includes freeing oppressor sectors on top who are the minority groups which exercise a disproportion of control in the global arena. When the people at the bottom redistribute God's wealth equally and democratically, the minority at the top are freed from the sin of hoarding the majority of the wealth. Put differently, the powerful elite of every country will then become the children of God who are simply equal to everyone else.

Furthermore, for black theology, the African American church is one of two main institutions—the other is the black family—that have the resources, moral authority, the oldest justice tradition, the broadest influence, and the place where most people expect to hear a healing and liberating word from God. By working as a prophetic part of the African American church and other faith communities, black theology of liberation can play a significant role in bringing about the new common wealth of the future. Out of the particularity of African American experiences, we embrace a new human community for all races and peoples.

NOTES

CHAPTER 1
BLACK THEOLOGY OF LIBERATION AND THE IMPACT OF WOMANIST THEOLOGY

1. New York: Harcourt Brace Jovanovich, 1983, pp. xi-xii.
2. "Black Theology and the Black Woman," in *Black Theology: A Documentary History, 1966-1979*, ed. Gayraud S. Wilmore and James H. Cone (Maryknoll, NY: Orbis Books, 1979), p. 423.
3. Found in *Feminist Interpretation of the Bible* (Westminster Press, 1985), p. 40.
4. Linda E. Thomas, "Womanist Theology, Epistemology, and a New Anthropological Paradigm," *Journal of Constructive Theology* (Centre for Constructive Theology, University of Durban-Westville, Durban, South Africa), vol. 2, no. 2, December 1996, pp. 19-31.
5. Delores Williams, "Womanist Theology: Black Women's Voices," in *Black Theology: A Documentary History Volume 2, 1980-1992*, ed. James H. Cone and Gayraud S. Wilmore (Maryknoll, NY: Orbis Books, 1993), p. 269.
6. Thomas, "Womanist Theology", pp. 19-32.
7. Thomas, pp. 19-32. Thomas is a professor of theology and anthropology at the Lutheran School of Theology at Chicago, where she conducts a comparative study between poor black Christian women in the south side of Chicago and those in townships in South Africa. She combines the commitment of her Christian witness (she is an ordained United Methodist clergywoman) with the scientific ethnographic techniques of fieldwork.

   In the article quoted she elaborates in detail the specific steps needed for womanists to use in actually being with poor black women in their communities and churches.
8. Emilie M. Townes, introduction to *A Troubling in My Soul: Womanist Perspectives on Evil and Suffering*, ed. Emilie M. Townes (Maryknoll, NY: Orbis Books, 1993), 2.

9.   Teresa L. Fry, "Avoiding Asphyxiation: A Womanist Perspective on Intrapersonal and Interpersonal Transformation," in *Embracing the Spirit: Womanist Perspectives on Hope, Salvation, and Transformation* (Maryknoll, NY: Orbis Books, 1997), ed. Emilie M. Townes, chapter 6. All references to Fry's work are from her article.

CHAPTER 2
THE PREFERENTIAL OPTION FOR THE POOR
AND THE OPPRESSED

1.   Gustavo Gutierrez, *A Theology of Liberation: History, Politics and Salvation* (Maryknoll, NY: Orbis Books, 1973), pp. 292-293.

2.   Charles L. Perdue Jr., Thomas E. Barden, and Robert K. Phillips, eds., *Weevils in the Wheat: Interview with Virginia Ex-Slaves* (Charlottesville, VA: University of Virginia Press, 1997), p. 94.

3.   John W. Blassingame, ed., *Slave Testimony: Two Centuries of Letters, Speeches, Interviews, and Autobiographies* (Baton Rouge, LA: Louisiana State University Press, 1977), p. 661.

4.   Mark Miles Fisher, *Negro Slave Songs in the United States* (Secaucus, NJ: The Citadel Press, 1978), p. 121.

5.   Martin Luther King Jr., "The President's Address to the Tenth Anniversary Convention of the Southern Christian Leadership Conference, Atlanta, Georgia, August 16, 1967," in *The Rhetoric of Black Power*, ed. Robert L. Scott and Wayne Brockriede (New York: Harper & Row, 1969), p. 161.

6.   James H. Cone, "Black Theology and the Black Church: Where Do We Go from Here?" in *Black Theology: A Documentary History, 1966-1979*, ed. Gayraud S. Wilmore and James H. Cone (Maryknoll, NY: Orbis Books, 1979), p. 358.

7.   The following three-part definition of poverty can be found in Gutierrez, *Theology of Liberation*, pp. 288-299.

8.   Ibid., pp. 291-296.

9.   Ibid., pp. 307-308.

10. Gustavo Gutierrez, *We Drink From Our Own Wells: The Spiritual Journey of a People* (Maryknoll, NY: Orbis Books, 1984), p. 2.

11. Cornel West, *Race Matters* (Boston, MA: Beacon Press, 1993), pp. 5-6.

12. David Ashley, *History Without a Subject: The Postmodern Turn* (Boulder, CO: Westview Press, 1997), p. 168.

13. I'd like to thank my research assistant, Kurt Buhring, for reorganizing the content of this chapter.

CHAPTER 3
SPIRITUALITY AND TRANSFORMATION
IN BLACK THEOLOGY

1. See "Dr. Martin Luther King, Jr., Speech at Staff Retreat Penn Center, Frogmore, South Carolina, May 23-31, 1967," p. 4 (author's copy). Other quotes by King are taken from his *The Trumpet of Conscience* (New York: Harper & Row, 1967), pp. 59-60; "The President's Address to the Tenth Anniversary Convention of the Southern Christian Leadership Conference, Atlanta, Georgia, August 16, 1967," in *The Rhetoric of Black Power,* ed. Robert L. Scott and Wayne Brockriede (New York: Harper & Row, 1969), pp. 162 and 155; and from David J. Garrow, *Bearing the Cross: Martin Luther King, Jr. and the Southern Christian Leadership Conference* (New York: William Morrow, 1986), pp. 364 and 537.

2. All of Toni Morrison's quotes are from Toni Morrison, *Beloved* (New York: New American Library, 1987). For a fuller treatment on Baby Suggs and the spirituality of the body, see pp. 87-89.

3. Charles L. Perdue Jr., Thomas E. Barden, and Robert K. Phillips, eds., *Weevils in the Wheat: Interviews with Virginia Ex-Slaves* (Bloomington: Indiana University Press, 1980), p. 100.

4. Clifton H. Johnson, ed., *God Struck Me Dead: Religious Conversion Experiences and Autobiographies of Ex-Slaves* (Philadelphia: Pilgrim Press, 1969), p. 14.

CHAPTER 4
A NEW BLACK HETEROSEXUAL MALE

1. Most group members belong to Trinity United Church of Christ in Chicago, Illinois. The senior pastor of Trinity, Jeremiah A. Wright Jr., initiated the idea of black Christian men's cell groups.

CHAPTER 5
A BLACK AMERICAN PERSPECTIVE ON INTERFAITH DIALOGUE
IN THE ECUMENICAL ASSOCIATION OF THIRD WORLD THEOLO-
GIANS

1. Gustavo Gutierrez, "Two Theological Perspectives: Liberation Theology and Progressivist Theology," in *The Emergent Gospel: Theology from the*

Underside of History, ed. Sergio Torres and Virginia Fabella (Maryknoll, NY: Orbis Books, 1978), p. 241.

2. Ibid.

3. Aloysius Pieris, *An Asian Theology of Liberation* (Maryknoll, NY: Orbis Books, 1988), p. 87.

4. Esau Tuza, "The Demolition of Church Buildings by the Ancestors," in *The Gospel Is Not Western: Black Theologies from the Southwest Pacific,* ed. G. W. Trompf (Maryknoll, NY: Orbis Books, 1987), p. 84.

5. Pieris, *Asian Theology,* p. 70.

6. Gabriel M. Setiloane, *African Theology: An Introduction* (Johannesburg, South Africa: Skotaville Publishers, 1986), p. 40.

7. Manuel M. Marzal, "The Religion of the Andean Quechua in Southern Peru," in *The Indian Face of God in Latin America,* ed. M. M. Marzal, E. Maurer, X. Albo, and B. Melia (Maryknoll, NY: Orbis Books, 1996), p. 69.

8. Ruth M. Stone, "Bringing the Extraordinary into the Ordinary: Music Performance among the Kpelle of Liberia," in *Religion in Africa,* ed. Thomas D. Blakely, Walter E. A. van Beek, and Dennis L. Thomson (Portsmouth, NH: Heinemann, 1994), p. 392.

9. Aruru Matiabe, "General Perspective: A Call for Black Humanity to Be Better Understood," in *The Gospel Is Not Western: Black Theologies from the Southwest Pacific,* ed. G. W. Trompf (Maryknoll, NY: Orbis Books, 1987), p. 17.

10. Quoted in V. T. Rajshekar, *Dalit: The Black Untouchables of India* (Atlanta, GA: Clarity Press, 1987), p. 41.

11. Ibid., p. 54.

12. Rosario Battung, "Indigenous People's Primal Religions and Cosmic Spirituality as Wellsprings of Life," in *Springs of Living Water,* ed. Marlene Perera, A. Nunuk P., and Murniati (Nagasandra, Bangalore: St. Paul's Press for the EATWOT, 1997), p. 121.

13. Eugenio Maurer, "Tseltal Christianity," in *The Indian Face of God in Latin America* ed. M. M. Marzel, E. Maurrer, X. Albo, and B. Melia (Maryknoll, NY: Orbis Books, 1996), p. 25.

14. Anne Pattel-Gray, *Through Aboriginal Eyes: The Cry from the Wilderness* (Geneva: World Council of Churches, 1991), pp. 6-7.

CHAPTER 6
THE RELIGION OF GLOBALIZATION

1. The web site of the Pluralism Project is: www.fas.harvard.edu\pluralism.

2. I am a member of the board of trustees of the Council for a Parliament of the World's Religions, chair of the international theological commission of the Ecumenical Association of Third World Theologians (EATWOT), and was a delegate to the eighth assembly of the World Council of Churches held in Harare, Zimbabwe, in December 1998. Documentation on the World Council of Churches and the Parliament can be obtained from the World Council of Churches, 150 Route de Ferney, P.O. Box 2100, 1211 Geneva 2, Switzerland and the Council for a Parliament of the World's Religions, P.O. Box 1630, Chicago, IL 60690 (web site: www.cpwr.org). For a detailed sociological and theological genealogy of EATWOT, see my *Introducing Black Theology of Liberation* (Maryknoll, NY: Orbis Books, 1999); James H. Cone, *For My People: Black Theology and the Black Church, Where Have We Been and Where are We Going?* (Maryknoll, NY: Orbis Books, 1984); and Theo Witvliet, *A Place in the Sun: An Introduction to Liberation Theology in the Third World* (Maryknoll, NY: Orbis Books, 1985).

3. Mary John Mananzan, a Filipina member of EATWOT, writes the following about globalization: "EATWOT theologians see Globalization as a new religion that has its dogma (profit), its ethical principles (laws of the market), its prophets and high priests (International Monetary Fund-World Bank, Trans National Corporations), its temples (Megamalls), its rituals (stock market biddings), its altar (market), its victims for sacrifice (greater majority of excluded peoples)." See her "Five Hundred Years of Colonial History: A Theological Reflection on the Philippine Experience" *Voices From the Third World*, vol. 21, no. 1, June 1998, p. 242.

   For definitions of religion, see Peter Beyer, *Religion and Globalization* (Thousand Oaks, CA: Sage, 1994), p. 5; and Paul Tillich, *Systematic Theology*, vol. I (Chicago: University of Chicago Press, 1951).

4. Nicholas D. Kristof with Edward Wyatt, "Who Sank, or Swam, in Choppy Currents of a World Cash Ocean," in *New York Times*, February 15, 1999.

5. Quoted from J. B. Banawiratma, "Religions in Indonesian Pluralistic Society in the Era of Globalization: A Christian Perspective" *Voices From the Third World*, vol. 22, no. 1, June 1999, p. 38.

6. See *Forbes*, October 12, 1998, p. 4, and *As the South Goes*, vol. 6, no. 1, Spring 1999 (a publication of the Institute for the Elimination of Poverty and Genocide, 9 Gammon Ave. S. W., Atlanta, GA. 30315).

7. Israel Batista, "Social Movements: A Personal Testimony," in *Social Movements, Globalization, Exclusion. Social Movements: Challenges and*

Perspectives, ed. Israel Batista (Geneva: World Council of Churches, 1967), p. 3.

8. Neoliberalism pursues its project just as aggressively in Europe, the former Eastern Bloc, and the remaining socialist countries. I underscore the Third World primarily because it combines to include the largest human and ecological resources in the world.

9. Carmelita M. Usog, "Doing Theology: Contextualized Theology (God-Talk, Women Speak)," *Voices from the Third World,* vol. 21, no. 1, June 1998, p. 197.

10. C. T. Kurien, "Globalization—What Is It About?" *Voices from the Third World,* vol. 20, no. 2, December 1997, p. 20.

11. See Zygmunt Bauman, "Introduction," in *Globalization: The Human Consequences* (New York: Columbia University Press, 1998); and Malcolm Waters, *Globalization* (New York: Routledge, 1995), chapter 3.

12. *Time,* November 9, 1998, p. 36.

13. Saskia Sassen, *Globalization and Its Discontents* (New York: The New Press, 1998), pp. xxii-xxiii.

14. Ana Maria Ezcurra, "Globalization, Neoliberalism and Civil Society," in *Social Movements, Globalization, Exclusion. Social Movements: Challenges and Perspectives,* ed. Israel Batista, (Geneva: World Council of Churches, 1997), p. 82.

15. K. C. Abraham, "Together in Mission and Unity: Beholding the Glory of God's Kingdom," *Voices from the Third World,* vol. 22, no. 2, June 1999, p. 144.

BIBLIOGRAPHY

This bibliography represents some of the major topics discussed in *Heart and Head*. The purpose is to point the reader in directions for further study.

BLACK THEOLOGY OF LIBERATION

Coleman, Will. *Tribal Talk: Black Theology, Hermeneutics, and African/American Ways of "Telling the Story."* University Park, PA: Pennsylvania State University Press, 2000.

Cone, James H. *Black Theology and Black Power.* Maryknoll, NY: Orbis Books, 1989. (Originally by Seabury Press, 1969.)

———. *For My People: Black Theology and the Black Church: Where Have We Been and Where Are We Going.* Maryknoll, NY: Orbis Books, 1984.

———. *A Black Theology of Liberation.* Maryknoll, NY: Orbis Books, 1990. (Originally by Seabury Press, 1970.)

———, and Gayraud S. Wilmore, eds., *Black Theology: A Documentary History,* vol. I: 1966-1979 and vol. II: 1980-1992. Maryknoll, NY: Orbis Books, 1993.

Hopkins, Dwight N. *Down, Up, and Over: Slave Religion and Black Theology.* Minneapolis, MN: Fortress Press, 1999.

———. *Introducing Black Theology of Liberation.* Maryknoll, NY: Orbis Books, 1999.

———. *Shoes That Fit Our Feet: Sources for a Constructive Black Theology.* Maryknoll, NY: Orbis Books, 1993.

———. and Linda E. Thomas. "Black Theology USA Revisited," *Journal of Theology for Southern Africa.* University of Cape Town, Cape Town, South Africa. March 1998.

———. "Voices from the Margins in the United States," in *The Twentieth Century: A Theological Overview,* ed. Gregory Baum. Maryknoll, NY: Orbis Books, 1999.

Wilmore, Gayraud S. and James H. Cone, eds., Black Theology A Documentary History, 1966-1979. Maryknoll, NY: Orbis Books, 1979.

WOMANIST THEOLOGY

Baker-Fletcher, Karen and Garth Baker-Fletcher. *My Sister, My Brother: Womanist and Xodus God-Talk.* Maryknoll, NY: Orbis Books, 1997.

Cannon, Katie. "The Emergence of Black Feminist Consciousness," in *Feminist Interpretation of the Bible,* ed. Letty M. Russell. Louisville, KY: Westminster Press, 1985.

Douglas, Kelly Brown. *The Black Christ.* Maryknoll, NY: Orbis Books, 1994.

Fry, Teresa L. "Avoiding Asphyxiation: A Womanist Perspective on Intrapersonal and Interpersonal Transformation," in *Embracing the Spirit: Womanist Perspectives on Hope, Salvation, and Transformation,* ed. Emilie M. Townes. Maryknoll, NY: Orbis Books, 1997.

Grant, Jacquelyn. "Womanist Theology: Black Women's Experience as a Source for Doing Theology, with Special Reference to Christology," *Journal of the Interdenominational Theological Center,* vol. 13, No. 2, Spring 1986.

Thomas, Linda E. "Womanist Theology, Epistemology, and a New Anthropological Paradigm," *Journal of Constructive Theology.* Centre for Constructive Theology, University of Durban-Westville, Durban, South Africa, vol. 2, no. 2, December 1996.

Townes, Emilie M. "Introduction," in *A Troubling in My Soul: Womanist Perspectives on Evil and Suffering,* ed. Emilie M. Townes. Maryknoll, NY: Orbis Books, 1993.

Walker, Alice. *In Search of Our Mothers' Gardens: Womanist Prose.* New York: Harcourt Brace Jovanovich, 1983.

POSTMODERNISM

Ashley, David. *History Without a Subject: The Postmodern Condition.* Boulder, CO: Westview Press, 1997.

Barker, Stephen, ed. *Signs of Change: Premodern—Modern—Postmodern.* Albany, NY: State University Press of New York, 1996.

Bertens, Hans. *The Idea of the Postmodern.* New York: Routledge, 1995.

Dickens, David R., and Andrea Fontana, eds. *Postmodernism & Social Inquiry.* New York: Guilford Press, 1994.

Docherty, Thomas, ed. *Postmodernism: A Reader.* New York: Columbia University Press, 1993.

Harvey, David. *The Condition of Postmodernity.* Cambridge, Massachusetts: Blackwell Publishers, 1995.

Jencks, Charles, ed. *The Post-Modern Reader.* New York: St. Martin's Press, 1992.

Lyotard, Jean Francois. *The Postmodern Condition: A Report on Knowledge.* Minneapolis, MN.: University of Minnesota Press, 1984.

Seidman, Steven, ed. *The Postmodern Turn: New Perspectives on Social Theory.* New York: Cambridge University Press, 1994.

LATIN AMERICAN LIBERATION THEOLOGY

Gutierrez, Gustavo. *Teologia de la liberacion, Perspectivas.* Lima, Peru: CEP, 1971.

———. *A Theology of Liberation: History, Politics and Salvation.* Maryknoll, NY: Orbis Books, 1973.

———. *We Drink From Our Own Wells: The Spiritual Journey of a People.* Maryknoll, NY: Orbis Books, 1984.

BLACK SPIRITUALITY

Blassingame, John W., ed. *Slave Testimony: Two Centuries of Letters, Speeches, Interviews, and Autobiographies.* Baton Rouge, LA: Louisiana State University Press, 1977.

Fisher, Mark Miles. *Negro Slave Songs in the United States.* Secaucus, NJ: The Citadel Press, 1978.

Johnson, Clifton H., ed. *God Struck Me Dead: Religious Conversion Experiences and Autobiographies of Ex-Slaves.* Philadelphia, PA: Pilgrim Press, 1969.

King, Martin Luther, Jr. "Dr. Martin Luther King, Jr. Speech at Staff Retreat Penn Center, Frogmore, South Carolina, May 23-31, 1967," author's copy.

———. *The Trumpet of Conscience.* New York: Harper & Row, 1967.

———. "The President's Address to the Tenth Anniversary Convention of the Southern Christian Leadership Conference, Atlanta, Georgia, August 16, 1967," in *Rhetoric of Black Power,* ed. Robert L. Scott and Wayne Brockriede. New York: Harper & Row, 1969.

Morrison, Toni. *Beloved.* New York: American Library, 1987.

Perdue, Charles L., Jr. Thomas E. Barden, and Robert K. Phillips, eds. *Weevils in the Wheat: Interview with Virginia Ex-Slaves.* Charlottesville, VA: University of Virginia Press, 1997.

BLACK MALES

Baker-Fletcher, Garth. *Xodus: An African American Male Journey.* Minneapolis, MN: Fortress Press, 1996.

Blount, Marcelus, and George P. Cunningham, eds. *Representing Black Men.* New York: Routledge, 1996.

Cone, James H. "Black Theology, Black Churches, and Black Women," in *For My People: Black Theology and the Black Church.* Maryknoll, NY: Orbis Books, 1984.

Elmore, Ronn. *How to Love a Black Woman.* New York: Warner Books, 1998.

Evans, James H. "Black Theology and Black Feminism," *Journal of Religious Thought.* vol. 38, no. 1, Spring-Summer, 1981.

Grier, William H. and Price M. Cobbs. *Black Rage.* New York: Basic Books, 1968.

Griffin, Horace. "Giving New Birth: Lesbians, Gays and the 'Family': A Pastoral Care Perspective," *Journal of Pastoral Theology,* Summer 1993.

———. Revisioning Christian Ethical Discourse on Homosexuality: A Challenge for the 21st Century," *Journal of Pastoral Care,* Summer 1999.

———. "Their Own Received Them Not: African American Lesbians and Gays in Black Churches," *Journal of Theology and Sexuality,* Spring 2000.

Harper, Phillip Brian. *Are We Not Men?: Masculine Anxiety and the Problem of African-American Identity.* New York: Oxford University Press, 1996.

Hopkins, Dwight N. "Black Women's Spirituality of Funk," in *Shoes That Fit Our Feet: Sources for a Constructive Black Theology.* Maryknoll, NY: Orbis Books, 1993.

Johnson, Ernest H. *Brothers on the Mend: Understanding and Healing Anger of African-American Men and Women.* New York: Pocket Books, 1998.

Majors, Richard, and Janet Mancini Billson, *Cool Pose: The Dilemmas of Black Manhood in America*. New York: Touchstone, 1992.

SEXUALITY

Frankenberg, Ruth. *White Women, Race Matters: The Social Construction of Whiteness*. Minneapolis, MN: University of Minnesota Press, 1993.

Guillaumin, Colette. *Racism, Sexism, Power and Ideology*. New York: Routledge, 1995.

Lancaster, Roger N., and Micaela di Leonardo, eds. *The Gender Sexuality Reader*. New York: Routledge, 1997.

McClintock, Anne. *Imperial Leather: Race, Gender and Sexuality in Colonial Conquest*. New York: Routledge, 1995.

Ortner, Sherry B. *Making Gender: The Politics and Erotics of Culture*. Boston, MA: Beacon Press, 1996.

Pile, Steve, and Nigel Thrift, eds. *Mapping the Subject: Geographies of Cultural Transformation*. New York: Routledge, 1995.

Stecopoulor, Harry, and Michael Uebel, eds. *Race and the Subject of Masculinities*. Durham, NC: Duke University Press, 1997.

Young, Robert J. C. *Colonial Desire: Hybridity in Theory, Culture and Race*. New York: Routledge, 1995.

THE INDIVIDUAL AND COLLECTIVE SELF

Barnes, Jonathan. *The Presocratic Philosophers*. New York: Routledge, 1993.

Chalmers, David J. *The Conscious Mind: In Search of a Fundamental Theory*. New York: Oxford University Press, 1996.

Critchley, Simon, and William R. Schroeder, eds. *A Companion to Continental Philosophy*. Malden, MA: Blackwell Publishers, 1999.

Eze, Emmanuel Chukwudi. *African Philosophy: An Anthology*. Malden, MA: Blackwell Publishers, 1998.

———. ed. *Postcolonial African Philosophy: A Critical Reader*. Malden, MA: Blackwell Publishers, 1997.

Coetzee, P. H., and A. P. J. Roux, eds. *The African Philosophy Reader*. New York: Routledge, 1998.

Flew, Anthony. *An Introduction to Western Philosophy: Ideas and Argument from Plato to Popper*. Revised edition. New York: Thames and Hudson, 1989.

Gay, Peter. *The Enlightenment: An Interpretation.* New York: Vintage, 1968.

Olupona, Jacob, ed. *African Traditional Religions in Contemporary Society.* New York: Paragon House, 1991.

Serequeberhan, Tsenay, ed. *African Philosophy: The Essential Readings.* New York: Paragon House, 1991.

WEALTH

Aldrich, Nelson W. *Old Money: The Mythology of America's Upper Class.* New York: A. A. Knopf, 1988.

Andrews, Marcellus. *The Political Economy of Hope and Fear: Capitalism and the Black Condition in America.* New York: New York University Press, 1999.

Conley, Dalton. *Being Black, Living in the Red: Race, Wealth, and Social Policy in America.* Berkeley, CA: University of California Press, 1999.

Oliver, Melvin L., and Thomas M. Shapiro, *Black Wealth/White Wealth: A New Perspective on Racial Inequality.* New York: Routledge, 1995.

RACE

Allen, James, ed. *Without Sanctuary: Lynching Photography in America.* Santa Fe, NM: Twin Palms Publishers, 2000.

Baker, Lee D. *From Savage to Negro: Anthropology and the Construction of Race, 1896-1954.* Berkeley, CA: University of California Press, 1998.

Barner, Annie. *Say It Loud: Middle-Class Blacks Talk about Racism and What to Do about It.* Cleveland, OH: Pilgrim Press, 2000.

Cassuto, Leonard. *The Inhuman Race: The Racial Grotesque in American Literature and Culture.* New York: Columbia University Press, 1997.

Gossett, Thomas F. *Race: The History of an Idea in America.* New York: Schocken Books, 1971.

Pattillo-McCoy, Mary *Black Picket Fences, Privileges and Peril among the Black Middle Class.* Chicago, IL: University of Chicago Press, 1999.

Pounds, Michael C. *Race in Space.* Lanham, MD: Scarecrow Press, 1999.

Turner, Patricia. *Ceramic Uncles and Celluloid Mammies: Black Images and Their Influence in Culture.* New York: Anchor Books, 1994.

West, Cornel. *Race Matters.* Boston, MA: Beacon Press, 1993.

INTERFAITH AND INTER-RELIGIOUS DIALOGUE

Battung, Rosario. "Indigenous People's Primal Religious and Cosmic Spirituality as Wellsprings of Life," in *Springs of Living Water,* ed. Marlene Perera and A. Nunuk P. Murniati. Nagasandra, Bangalore: St. Paul's Press for EATWOT, 1997.

Bimwemyi, Oscar K. "A l'origine de l'association oecumenique des theologiens du Tiers Monde," *Bulletin de Theologie Africaine,* vol. 2, no. 3, January-June 1980.

Cone, James H. "Ecumenical Association of Third World Theologians," *Ecumenical Trends,* vol. 14, no. 8, September 1985.

Gutierrez, Gustavo. "Two Theological Perspectives: Liberation Theology and Progressivist Theology," in *The Emergent Gospel: Theology from the Underside of History,* ed. Sergio Torres and Virginia Fabella. Maryknoll, NY: Orbis Books, 1978.

Marzal, Manuel M. "The Religion of the Andean Quechua in Southern Peru," in *The Indian Face of God in Latin America,* ed. M. M. Marzal, Eugenio Maurer, Xavier Albo, and Bertome Melia. Maryknoll, NY: Orbis Books, 1996.

Matiabe, Aruru. "General Perspective: A Call for Black Humanity to Be Better Understood," in *The Gospel Is Not Western: Black Theologies from the Southwest Pacific,* ed. G. W. Trompf. Maryknoll, NY: Orbis Books, 1987.

Maurer, Eugenio. "Tseltal Christianity," in *The Indian Face of God in Latin America.* Maryknoll, NY: Orbis Books, 1996.

Pattel-Gray, Anne. *Through Aboriginal Eyes: The Cry from the Wilderness.* Geneva: World Council of Churches, 1991.

Pieris, Aloysius. *An Asian Theology of Liberation.* Maryknoll, NY: Orbis Books, 1988.

———. "Towards an Asian Theology of Liberation: Some Religio-Cultural Guidelines," in *Asia's Struggle for Full Humanity,* ed. Virginia Fabella. Maryknoll, NY: Orbis Books, 1980.

Rajshekar, V. T. *Dalit: The Black Untouchables of India.* Atlanta, GA: Clarity Press, 1987.

Setiloane, Gabriel M. *African Theology: An Introduction.* Johannesburg, South Africa: Skotaville Press, 1986.

Stone, Ruth M. "Bringing the Extraordinary into the Ordinary: Music Perfor-mance among the Kpelle of Liberia," in *Religion in Africa,* ed. Thomas D. Blakely, Walter E. A. van Beek, and Dennis L. Thomson. Portsmouth, NH: Heinemann, 1994.

Tuza, Esau. "The Demolition of Church Buildings by the Ancestors," in *The Gospel Is Not Western: Black Theologies from the Southwest Pacific,* ed. G. W. Trompf. Maryknoll, NY: Orbis Books, 1987.

GLOBALIZATION

Amin, Samir. *Re-Reading the Postwar Period: An Intellectual Itinerary.* New York: Monthly Review Press, 1994.

Appadurai, Arjun. *Modernity at Large: Cultural Dimensions of Globalization.* Minneapolis, MN: University of Minnesota Press, 1996.

Batista, Israel, ed. *Social Movements, Globalization, Exclusion: Social Movements, Challenges and Perspectives.* Geneva: World Council of Churches, 1997.

Bauman, Zygmunt. *Globalization: The Human Consequences.* New York: Columbia University Press, 1998.

Beyer, Peter. *Religion and Globalization.* Thousand Oaks, CA: Sage, 1994. Clark Wade Roof, ed. *World Order and Religion.* Albany, NY: State University of New York Press, 1991.

Duchrow, U. *Alternatives to Global Capitalism: Drawn from Biblical History, Designed for Political Action.* Utrecht: International Books, 1995.

Featherstone, Mike, Scott Lash, and Roland Robertson, eds. *Global Modernities.* Thousand Oaks, CA: Sage, 1995.

Hexhma, Irving, and Karla Poewe. *Making the Human Sacred: New Religions as Global Cultures.* Boulder, CO: Westview Press, 1997.

Hoeber, Susanne Rudolph, and James Piscatori, eds. *Transnational Religion and Fading States.* Boulder, CO: Westview Press, 1997.

Kurien, C. T. "Globalization—What Is It About?" in *Voices from the Third World,* vol. 20, no. 2, December 1997.

Mananzan, Mary John. "Five Hundred Years of Colonial History: A Theological Reflection on the Philippine Experience," in *Voices from the Third World,* vol. 21, no. 1, June 1998.

"Report of the Ecumenical Association of Third World Theologians Evaluation Commission," in *Voices from the Third World,* vol. 19, no. 2, December 1996.

Robertson, Roland. *Globalization: Social Theory and Global Culture.* Thousand Oaks, CA: Sage, 1992.

Sassen, Saskia. *Globalization and Its Discontents: Essays on the New Mobility of People and Money.* New York: The New Press, 1998.

Schreiter, Robert J. *The New Catholicity: Theology Between the Global and the Local.* Maryknoll, NY: Orbis Books, 1997.

Swamy, Dalip. "An Alternative to Globalization," in *Voices from the Third World,* vol. 20, no. 1, June 1997.

Swatos, William H., ed. *Religious Politics in Global Perspective.* New York: Greenwood Press, 1989.

Waters, Malcolm. *Globalization.* New York: Routledge, 1995.

Witte, John, Jr., and Johan D. van der Vyver, eds. *Religious Human Rights in Global Perspective: Religious Perspectives.* Boston: Martinus Nijhoff Publishers, 1996.

CHRISTIANITY AND INDIGENOUS RELIGIONS

Banawiratma, J. B. "Religions in Indonesian Pluralistic Society in the Era of Globalization: A Christian Perspective," in *Voices from the Third World,* vol. 22, no. 1, June 1999.

Beyer, Peter. *Religion and Globalization.* Thousand Oaks, CA: Sage, 1994.

Long, Charles H. *Significations: Signs, Symbols, and Images in the Interpretation of Religion.* Minneapolis, MN: Fortress Press, 1986.

Tillich, Paul. *Systematic Theology, Vol. I.* Chicago, IL: University of Chicago Press, 1951.

Tinker, Tink *Missionary Conquest: The Gospel of Native American Cultural Genocide.* Minneapolis, MN: Fortress Press, 1993.

THEOLOGY AND THEOLOGICAL ANTHROPOLOGY

Blakely, Thomas D., Walter E. A. van Beek, and Dennis L. Thomson, eds. *Religion in Africa.* Portsmouth, NH: Heinemann, 1994.

Hanson, Bradley C. *Introduction to Christian Theology.* Minneapolis, MN: Fortress Press, 1997.

Hodgson Peter C., and Robert H. King, eds. *Christian Theology: An Introduction to Its Traditions and Tasks.* MN, Minnesota: Fortress Press, 1985.

Lawson, E. Thomas. *Religions of Africa.* San Francisco, CA: Harper & Row, 1985.

Magesa, Laurenti. *African Religion: The Moral Traditions of Abundant Life.* Maryknoll, NY: Orbis Books, 1997.

Mbiti, John. *African Religions and Philosophy.* Garden City, NY: Anchor Books, 1970.

———. *Introduction to African Religion.* Portsmouth, NH: Heinemann, 1975.

McGrath, Alister E. *Christian Theology: An Introduction.* Cambridge, MA: Blackwell, 1994.

Serequeberhan, Tsenay, ed. *African Philosophy: The Essential Writings.* New York: Paragon House, 1991.

NEOLIBERALISM

Abraham, K. C. "Together in Mission and Unity: Beholding the Glory of God's Kingdom," in *Voices from the Third World,* vol. 22, no. 2, June 1999.

Amin, Samir. *Re-Reading the Postwar Period: An Intellectual Itinerary.* New York: Monthly Review Press, 1994.

Batista, Israel. ed. *Social Movements, Globalization, Exclusion: Social Movements, Challenges and Perspectives.* Geneva: World Council of Churches, 1997.

Kurian, V. Matthew. "Evolution of the Market and Its Social Implications," in *Voices from the Third World,* vol. 21, no. 1, June 1998.

McIsaac, Peter. "Structural Adjustment Programmes: Capitalist Myth in Africa," in *Voices from the Third World,* vol. 21, no. 1, June 1998.

Usog, Carmelita M. "Doing Theology: Contextualized Theology. (God-Talk, Women Speak," in *Voices from the Third World,* vol. 21, no. 1, June 1998.

THE BIBLE

Bailey, Randall C. and Jacquelyn Grant, eds. *The Recovery of Black Presence: An Interdisciplinary Exploration.* Nashville, TN: Abingdon Press, 1995.

"Biblical Literature, the King James and Subsequent Versions," in *Encyclopedia Britannica* online, www.britannica.com.

Coote, Robert B. and Mary P. Coote, *Power, Politics, and the Making of the Bible: An Introduction.* Minneapolis, MN: Fortress Press, 1990.

Felder, Cain Hope. *Troubling Biblical Waters: Race, Class, and Family.* Maryknoll, NY: Orbis Books, 1989.

————, ed. *Stony the Road We Trod: African American Biblical Interpretation.* Minneapolis, MN: Fortress Press, 1991.

Friedman, Richard Elliott. *Who Wrote the Bible?* New York: Harper & Row, 1987.

Gomes, Peter J. *The Good Book: Reading the Bible with Mind and Heart.* New York: Avon Books, 1996.

THEOLOGY AND CLASS, GENDER,
SEXUAL ORIENTATION, SPIRITUALITY,
AND ECOLOGY

Ali, Carroll A. Watkins. *Survival and Liberation: Pastoral Theology in Africa American Context.* St. Louis, MO: Chalice Press, 1999.

Baker-Fletcher, Karen. *Sisters of Dust, Sisters of Spirit: Womanist Wordings on God and Creation.* Minneapolis, MN: Fortress Press, 1998.

Cannon, Katie Geneva. "Racism and Economics: The Perspective of Oliver C. Cox," in *Katie's Canon: Womanism and the Soul of the Black Community.* New York: Continuum, 1995.

Cone, James H. "Black Theology, Black Churches, and Black Women," in *For My People: Black Theology and the Black Church.* Maryknoll, NY: Orbis Books, 1984.

————. "Whose Earth Is It, Anyway? 1998," in *Risks of Faith: The Emergence of a Black Theology of Liberation, 1968-1998.* Boston, MA: Beacon Press, 1999.

Davis, Angela Y. *Women, Race, Class, and Gender.* New York: Random House, 1981.

Kelly Brown Douglas, *Sexuality and the Black Church.* Maryknoll, NY: Orbis Books, 1999.

Evans, James H. "Black Theology and Black Feminism," *Journal of Religious Thought,* vol. 38, no. 1, Spring-Summer 1981.

Farajaje-Jones, Elias. "Breaking Silence: Toward an in-the-Life Theology," in *Black Theology: A Documentary History Vol. II, 1980-1992,* ed. James H. Cone and Gayraud S. Wilmore. Maryknoll, NY: Orbis Books, 1993.

Giddens, Paula. *When and Where I Enter: The Impact of Black Women on Race, Class, and Gender.* New York: Random House, 1981.

Hill, Renee. "Who Are We for Each Other?: Sexism, Sexuality and Womanist Thought," in *Black Theology: A Documentary History Vol. II, 1980-1992,* ed. James H. Cone and Gayraud S. Wilmore. Maryknoll, NY: Orbis Books, 1993.

Hopkins, Dwight N. "Black Women's Spirituality of Funk," in *Shoes That Fit Our Feet: Sources for a Constructive Black Theology*. Maryknoll, NY: Orbis Books, 1993.

———. "Malcolm and Martin: To Change the World," in ibid.

Lartey, Emmanuel Y. *In Living Colour: An Intercultural Approach to Pastoral Care and Counseling*. Herndon, VA: Cassell, 1997.

Riggs, Marcia Y. *Awake, Arise and Act: A Womanist Call for Black Liberation*. Cleveland, OH: Pilgrim Press, 1994.

Robers, J. Deotis. *Roots of the Black Future: Family and Church*. Philadelphia, PA: Westminster Press, 1980.

Sanders, Cheryl J. "Christian Ethic and Theology in Womanist Perspective," in *Black Theology: A Documentary History, Vol. II, 1980-1992*, ed. James H. Cone and Gayraud S. Wilmore. Maryknoll, NY: Orbis Books, 1993.

Smith, Bill. "Liberation as Risky Business," in *Changing Conversations: Religious Reflection and Cultural Analysis*, ed. Dwight N. Hopkins and Sheila Greeve Davaney. New York: Routledge, 1996.

Terrell, JoAnne Marie. *Power in the Blood? The Cross in the African American Experience*. Maryknoll, NY: Orbis Books, 1998.

Thomas, Linda E. "Womanist Theology, Epistemology, and a New Anthropological Paradigm," *Journal of Constructive Theology*, vol. 1, no. 2, December 1996.

Townes, Emilie M. *Breaking the Fine Rain of Death: African American Health Issues and a Womanist Ethic of Care*. New York: Continuum, 1998.

West, Cornel. "Black Theology and Marxist Thought," in *Black Theology: A Documentary History Vol. I: 1966-1979*, ed. James H. Cone and Gayraud S. Wilmore. Maryknoll, NY: Orbis Books, 1993.

———. "Black Theology of Liberation as Critique of Capitalist Civilization," in *Black Theology: A Documentary History Vol. II: 1980-1992*, ed. James H. Cone and Gayraud S. Wilmore. Maryknoll, NY: Orbis Books, 1993.

West, Traci. *Wounds of the Spirit: Black Women, Violence, and Resistance Ethics*. New York: New York University Press, 1999.

White, Deborah Gray. *Ar'n't I A Woman? Female Slaves in the Plantation South*. New York: Norton, 1985.

Wimberly, Edward P. *African American Pastoral Care*. Nashville, TN: Abingdon Press, 1991.

————. *Counseling African American Marriages and Families.* Louisville, KY: Westminster John Knox Press, 1997.

INDEX

DATE DUE

#47-0108 Peel Off Pressure Sensitive